£1-99

G000153342

YORKSHIRE HUMOUR ON THE RAILS

BY

PETER KIRTON

© Copyright Peter Kirton 2003

No part may be reproduced
or copied in any form, in any language, whether by graphic,
visual, electronic, filming audio recording or any other means
without the prior written permission of the author

ISBN. 0-9546118-0-2

Published By
Write Books CPR Ltd
Pontefract Road
Ferrybridge
West Yorkshire
WF11 8PL

Dedication

*This book is dedicated to all retired
railway men and women*

Front & Rear Cover - Both photos kindly donated by FASTLINE
Photographic Ltd. Tel. 01904 522575

Front Cover : Leeds City Square 1958. Roof of old station can clearly be
seen rear centre of photograph.

Rear Cover : Leeds reborn. The new roof glistens over the rejuvenated
station 2002.

CONTENTS

More Going Loco

The Boss Is Hiding On Platform 12
Gordon Ambler
By The Lay By

I'm In Charge
Paul Opresco
More Of The World Outside

A Tale Of Two Cats?
Andy Stephenson
The Great British Public

Drinking On Duty?
Shirley Mitchell
Conveyance Of Passengers

A Stiff In The Loo
John Harrison
Clickety-click

You Boy, You Will Clean The Waiting Room
Ronnie Stead
The Deltics

Cholley's Stopped A Hot One
Gordon Reed
Anglo Scots

Romance At The Double
Peter Brooks
More Of Cova

Wor Abart That Woodbine Tha' Owes Mi?
Peter Kirton
The InterCity Era

The Royal Scot
Frank Geeson

The Nationalised era of Britain's railways was one of the most important periods in their history. Here are the veterans of British Rail, many of whom served throughout the period of its birth on the 1ˢᵗ January 1948 until the gradual demise into a privatised industry from 1994 onwards. For years it has been popular to criticise the way the railways are run and since privatisation the trend has probably increased. So, when we look back on the British Rail period we realise that in 1948 we took over a rail system that had been the country's internal lifeline throughout the Second World War (1939-1945). During this period the railways transported men and materials of the armed forces, the general public and virtually every commodity required by a nation to exist over those traumatic and demanding years.

At the time of Nationalisation much of the railways' hardware and infrastructure was in need of renewal and modernisation but as the country was virtually bankrupt we had to run a railway that had not changed much since the end of the Victorian era. Throughout the life of British Rail, it was never to receive the kind of investment required. When we look back and see what we did achieve with the equipment and tools we had, on reflection much of the credit of this unique period in railway history is down to the professionalism and dedication of the thousands of British Rail workers. Although often working in difficult and trying conditions, at all times of the day and night, they went about their duties with a camaraderie and a sense of humour which shines through in the following pages of the rail workers' own stories.

ACKNOWLEDGEMENTS

I am indebted to the following organisations, departments, libraries and people for their freely-volunteered help in many research matters and information: my sincere thanks.

Middleton Railway Trust

Leeds Reference Library

Railtrack and Network Rail

Integrated Electronic Control Centre, York

York Reference Library

Acomb Library

National Railway Museum

National Railway Museum Library Service

London North Western Railway Society

Great North Eastern Railway

FASTLINE Photographic Ltd.

Lisa Amos, Phil Atkins, Peter Brooks, George Case, Mustafa Cova, David Eyers, Steve Fountain, David Frodsham, Peter Goddard, Phil Graham, John Hanson, Stan Holdsworth, David Hughes, Denis Kidd, Norman Lee, Graham North, Peter Rose, Martin O'Shea, Vicky Samuels, Louis Scully, David Spink, Naomi Steer,

I would also say a special thank you to my two grandchildren Mark and Craig Allan, for their help in keeping my records straight and their help with the word processing.

I am also indebted to Peter Rose, a fellow member of the Leeds Branch of the British Rail Retired Staff Association, who has generously contributed some of his remarkable photos taken in the early 1960s.

A special thank you to all who have contributed to this book. They are listed in the order their stories appear:

Ian Sykes, Hugh Dick, David Eyers, Bob Oliver, Brian Marshall, Tom Hardy, Dennis Howson, Frank Edwards, M.B.E., Barrie Conlon, Bill Cunliffe, Graham Briggs, Joe Lomax, Ralph Waggett, Derrick Boden, Gordon Ambler, Paul Opresco, Andy Stephenson, Shirley Mitchell, John Harrison, Ronnie Stead, Gordon Reed and Peter Brooks.

A special thank you to my friend Patrick Howat for checking my text and for his expert advice and finally a thank you to my wife Maureen for once again giving me her support throughout this project.

11

Foreword

By Phil Graham

Area Operations Manager, Network Rail

Sit with any group of old railwaymen in a quiet period and you will always hear some tales. Meet a group of retired staff and you will hear even more. The tales are invariably about the job and to the layman, more interestingly, its social interaction. Why is this so? Well historically the railway has taken a 15-year-old boy (for a variety of reasons – often pure chance) and kept him until he retired half a century later. Early in that process the railway got into the blood and he was committed for life.

The railway used to employ such a variety of trades, professions and jobs, that many men changed direction without leaving their employer, while many more stayed in the same job for incredibly long periods. When I was a child I remember a signalman retiring in the mid 1960s after more than 40 years in the same, single-manned signal box. I bet he could have told some tales! I think that is the point. While I am sure he could tell an interesting tale or two, he, like many others, has been allowed to pass on and take his tales with him.

What Peter Kirton succeeds in doing in this book is to capture those tales for us, for all time and for a wider audience to enjoy. Nor was it easy. Tales that are told among colleagues in a mess-room or retired folk in a pub do not need any great literary skill or confidentiality. For a start, most of the 'audience' will know what the signal box or parcels office was like, how it smelt, where exactly it was, just what the Station Master was like etc. While these pages will be read by some who know some of the people and places, the vast majority will not. Not all will have worked on the railway. They need the scene painting – not too elaborately or it will become boring and not too thinly or the reader will not picture it correctly, but

12

just the right level of detail and some names have to be changed to protect the innocent! That is the skill that Peter has. He has proved it in the two volumes already published and for me, most graphically, in his own railway-life autobiography 'Proceed at Caution', which I just could not put down.

So what is this book about? More of the same? Well, yes, but much wider in scope. Peter has found no fewer than twenty-two other time-served railwaymen from different jobs, but all from the 'front line' and has helped them to tell the very best of each of their stories. In some cases those concerned possessed the necessary literary skills and were able to give Peter a manuscript. At the other end of the scale, but perhaps even more important, for all too often their stories perish with them, were those who needed to record their experiences on tape enabling Peter to write them in a form that all can understand, without any embellishment, just clarification: they remain the contributors' stories.

In nearly every case the contributors worked through the major social, economic and railway upheaval that was the 1960s. In some cases they actually worked in 'privatisation mark one' and some even survived into the present private railway. Changes in traction type, speed, places served, stations, goods and parcels traffic and signalling, not to mention public expectations, have far out-weighed the organisation and ownership changes that have spanned this period. In many cases (none more so than signalling) the old traditional methods survived, indeed some still do. Alongside the latest state-of-the-art systems, in a fascinating but incongruous medley and some contributors' stories could, therefore, have occurred half a century earlier than they actually did.

In most cases the tales are funny, some hysterically so (wait until you get Bob Oliver and the bees!) but while the humour may be what we all best remember, let us never forget that this was (and is) a service and a service to the whole community (not just the passengers), often carried out in a methodical, unassuming way and

13

for me I think of Ian Sykes and the runaway schoolgirl and my old friend Brian Marshall and the trespassing children at Kirkstall. Just think for a moment how differently those stories could (and probably would) have ended but for the dedication of railwaymen. (Interestingly, although I know these men and was once the manager of both, I learnt their stories first in these pages – unassuming? I think so.)

In between each railwayman's story, Peter has written a few paragraphs on certain elements of railway and social history, which serve to set the scene and explain the industry's development further.

It is with pleasure and pride that I write these words. Pleasure that I have known some of the storytellers, a joy to read all their stories and pride that after a mere 30 years' service, I must have become a railwayman, in order to be asked!

Long may the Leeds Retired Staff relate their tales live!

21st May 2003
Knaresborough
North Yorkshire.

THE LEEDS BRANCH, BRITISH RAIL RETIRED STAFF ASSOCIATION

In retirement my wife and I have regularly been to the over-50s swimming sessions at Tadcaster Swimming Pool. Although far from class swimmers, we do enjoy the exercise and the company of the regulars on these occasions. It so happens that Peter Brooks, retired Assistant Station Manager at Leeds Station, who lives in Leeds, also prefers the Tadcaster Swimming Pool. I had known Peter for many years but we lost touch after I took early retirement in November 1993. It was a real surprise when one day he came to our swimming session, and he has been a regular ever since. It did not take long for Peter to tell me about the Leeds Branch of the British Rail Staff Association and urge me to become a member. Well, I had spent a good period of my working life at Leeds - 20 years in fact from 1971 - so I considered myself well eligible to join this exclusive band of men and women.

The meetings are held at the B.R.S.A. Club at Skipton, just outside the railway station, on the last Thursday of every month. I first became a member in September 2001 and really enjoyed meeting up with and seeing old acquaintances I hadn't seen in years. Naturally, the main topic of conversation among the one hundred or so people who attend these meetings is railways! How did you ever guess? And as you pass the different groups on the way to the bar, you hear: 'do you remember the time when....?'

This retirement club was born on 14th April 1968 when four retired colleagues met in the refreshment room on Leeds City Station. They were Harry Greenwood, Allan Thwaite, Jack Sewell and Laury Turner, sadly, now all passed on. It is almost certain that this was the first of many retirement branches that was to follow all over the country. Harry Greenwood was later made a Life Member of the B.R.S.A. in recognition of his contribution to the Association. Unfortunately I only knew one of these founder members: Alan Thwaite, who was a signalling inspector and at one period was my boss when I was a young signalman. He had a strong North Yorkshire accent and I always considered him a gentleman. I well remember the time he came to pass me out to work my first main line signal box at Oakenshaw North Junction on the old Midland Railway. He watched me work the box for some time and then questioned me on the special instructions and I will always remember how he told me I had passed. 'Well lad. Ah think tha'll be al-reight. Think on and don't be doin owt daft, tha knows'. I'm pleased to say I didn't do owt daft, so did not let him down. Some signal inspectors would sneak up to the signal box to try and see if the signalman was doing anything incorrectly but Alan would always press his foot on the line-side signal wires, which then vibrated heavily in the lower floor of the signal box thus alerting the signalman that someone was approaching his box. Alan was well into his nineties before he decided to take his signalling skills to the railway in the sky, and I have no doubt that he will still tread on the signal wires to let the signalman know he is on his way!

It was through observing these retired staff with their wealth of knowledge of the railways that the thought struck me. When these people pass on, as for sure we all will, all the stories they are repeating to each other will be lost for ever. What a great pity, because the bulk of their service was while the railways were nationally owned from 1948 to 1994.

It was then that I decided to make the effort to collect some of these stories about some of the Leeds railwaymen and women who worked for British Rail, in many cases throughout their entire career, and put them together for posterity. I first of all sought permission for this project from the President, Bob Oliver, and the Secretary, who by now was Peter Brooks, both of whom gave me their approval and assistance. The next stage was not quite so easy. Its one thing to tell the tale of an incident when with old friends and having a few beers, but to ask someone to write it down for you the next day suddenly becomes a task they prefer not to bother with. Some people just do not like writing, others are embarrassed to record their stories on paper, and others think they do not have anything of interest to write. I eventually overcame this problem by taking my tape recorder to the meetings and having a friendly chat with people reluctant to put pen to paper. From these recordings I played and replayed the tapes till, I hope, I captured their stories as they wanted them told. I am indebted to all the people who have given me their time and contributed to this book, which without their help it would never have came about.

INTRODUCTION

What is a railway? Historically a railway is merely a road on which rails are laid. Originally the rails were of wood, stone or iron and were laid flat on the surface and vehicles with ordinary wheels were free to use the special track or to move at large over the whole width of the road. In the next stage of development, the rails were continuous iron plates with flanges on their outer edges to confine the wheels to the track proper. In the next stage, the rails were raised above the surface and the flange was transferred from the rails to the wheels. The railway thus became specialised; special vehicles could only use it and these vehicles could no longer be used on ordinary roads. The result was that the railway deserted the public highway and was laid on land allocated to its sole use.

The City of Leeds has much to thank the original Middleton Railway. Along a wagon way (oak rails, topped with a renewable strip of beech) it transported the cheap coal that fuelled the infant industries of iron and brass founding, pottery, glass and brick making. It also provided the first successful introduction of steam locomotives in moving wagonloads of coal and so was a major contributor to the industrial revolution.

It laid claim to be the world's first railway. The Leeds Intelligencer of Tuesday 26th September 1758 reported that:

> *On Wednesday last, the first wagonload of coals was brought from the pits of Charles Brandling Esq. down the new road to his staith near the bridge in this Town, agreeable to the Act of Parliament past last sessions. A scheme of such general utility, as to comprehend within it, not only our trade and poor, (which ought to be the grand objects of our concern) but also beneficial to every individual within this Town and Neighbourhood: On this occasion the bells were set a ringing, the cannons of our Fort fired, and a general joy appeared in every face.*

They may not have invented the wheel but the early engineers of the Middleton Railway were to show the world what could be done

18

with wheels on an iron rail. On the 24th June 1812 the first steam engine to run on a new iron wagon way was carried out. The Leeds Mercury reported that:

A highly interesting experiment was made with a machine constructed by Messrs Fenton, Murray and Wood of this place, under the direction of Mr John Blenkinsop, the Patentee, for the purpose of substituting the agency of steam for the use of horses in the conveyance of coals on the iron-rail-way from the mines of J C Brandling Esq, at Middleton to Leeds. This machine is, in fact a steam-engine of four horses' power, which, with the assistance of cranks turning a cog-wheel and iron cogs placed at one side of the rail-way is capable of moving, when lightly loaded, at the speed of ten miles an hour. At four o'clock in the afternoon, the machine ran from the coal-staith to the top of Hunslet-Moor, where six and afterwards eight wagons of coal, each weighing three tons, were hooked to the back part. With this immense weight, to which, as it approached the town, was super-added about 50 of the spectators mounted upon the wagons, it set off on its return journey to the coal-staith and performed the journey, a distance of about a mile and a half, principally on a dead level, in 23 minutes, without the slightest accident. The experiment, which was witnessed by thousands of spectators, was crowned with complete success and when it is considered that this invention is applicable to all rail-roads, and that upon the works of Mr Brandling alone, the use of 50 horses will be dispensed with, and the corn necessary for the consumption of, at least, 200 men saved, we cannot forbear to hail the invention as of vast public utility, and to rank the inventor amongst the benefactors of his country. The eight wagons of coals brought to Leeds at the launching of the machine, was by order of Mr Blenkinsop, presented to the General Infirmary.

Over 240 years later the Middleton Railway is still operating, providing steam enthusiasts with a taste of nostalgia and, to hundreds of school children each year, a taste of living history.

By the 1820s much of the area's woollen textiles were processed through Leeds and Wakefield and transported to the port of Hull for shipment to Europe. The means of moving the goods to Hull was a slow process by road or canal via Selby. The need for a much quicker mode of transport produced the building of the Leeds and Selby Railway, which was opened in 1834. Principally built to carry goods, with passengers a secondary consideration, it ran from Marsh Lane terminal station to a station at Selby where the wagons were run on to a wharf on the River Ouse. They were then loaded on to steam packets for the journey to Europe.

Towards the end of the 1830s, three more railways were approaching Leeds. The North Midland Railway ran from Derby to Leeds via Normanton with a terminal station at Hunslet Lane. George Hudson's York and North Midland Railway ran from York to the east of Leeds, where it joined the Leeds and Selby Railway at South Milford, then on to Castleford, joining the North Midland Railway at Altofts. The third was the Manchester and Leeds Railway, coming down the Calder Valley and joining the North Midland at Normanton to share the use of Hunslet Lane Station, until it eventually opened one of its own, near Wellington Street Leeds. All were fully operational by 1841.

This then was just the start of what was to be a chaotic period of emerging railway companies. They vied with each other for supremacy, especially in the West Riding of Yorkshire, where the developing coal industry provided fuel to start a flood of engineering industries and to consolidate the textile trade by building large factories in the towns. In retrospect, it was a ridiculous situation: where one railway company went, another would follow. Numerous towns and even villages had two stations, some even had three and still they fought in wasteful competition. More than seven railway companies were keen to exploit the vast potential of the West Riding of Yorkshire with Leeds at the hub of what was possibly the most complex railway system in Britain outside London.

Eventually after much argument, wrangling and inter-company rivalry, three stations would serve the needs of Leeds - there was even an argument about who should open one of the stations - Wellington Street, opened 1st July 1846, Central, opened 18th September 1848 and Leeds New which became operational on 1st April 1869.

The engineers were not slow to open up the potential of machinery; James Kitson of Hunslet built the famous 0-4-2 Lion, the first of six steam engines built for the Liverpool and Manchester Railway. The firm of Fenton, Murray & Jackson excelled in building twenty 7ft single 'Firefly' class express engines for the Great Western Railway. By the mid 1860s the Hunslet district of Leeds had arguably become one of the most intensive locomotive building centres in the world, and eventually, producing over 10,000 steam locomotives.

For well over fifty years the need for a single station was discussed but nothing ever came of these proposals until on the 2nd May 1938 when Wellington and New were connected and named City North and City South: combined Leeds City. A later report by the LMS and LNER stated that it was impracticable or uneconomic to combine the Leeds passenger stations but after nationalisation on the 1st January 1948 there was a determination to achieve this objective. Investment in British Railways was at a premium but in 1959 over four million pounds was made available for concentrating all passenger services at a rebuilt Leeds City. In 1961 the work stopped due to lack of funding and did not resume till 1963. With the final work complete, City North was converted to a parcels concentration depot (PCD) and the extensively enlarged City South, along with new track layouts and a new power signal box, became Leeds City on the 1st May 1967. The old Central Station closed the day before.

Unfortunately, by this time, Dr Beeching, the government appointed axe-man, was doing his duty and cutting out considerable routes and services on the whole of British Rail (changed from British Railways to British Rail in 1965) and the West Riding was to feel the pain more than most. Under-funding and the popularity of road transport plunged the railways into further decline. Following the 1968 Transport Act, in the early 1970s the government set up several Metropolitan County Councils, of which West Yorkshire covered Leeds and its environs. To oversee the transport policy of each area a Passenger Transport Authority was created and for the Leeds area known as the West Yorkshire Passenger Transport Executive (WYPTE).

Section 20 of the Transport Act that created the new Metropolitan County Councils also set the formal relationship between the Councils and British Railways. Agreements between the two parties were known as 'Section 20 agreements'. These agreements produced much-needed funding to a system that at one period seemed to be grinding to a halt. New trains were introduced, and improvements at virtually every station within West Yorkshire. Marketed under the name 'Metro', the PTE specified service levels and fares, but BR ran the services on its behalf. Between 1982 and 1992, more than 20 new stations were opened or reopened, and the passenger flow into Leeds was now 15 million per year!

The amount of goods traffic handled at Leeds was reflected in the number of depots. Four large sorting yards, nine freight sidings, a freightliner depot and an abundance of private sidings. Wellington Street, Hunslet Lane, Stourton, Copley Hill and Neville Hill handled the most traffic. In their heyday these yards were working 24 hours a day and many for seven days a week, and employing hundreds of staff. With so many different railway companies competing for the services emanating from the Leeds railway system, the number of engine sheds built to service the whole complex organisation was no wonder. Five sheds (Holbeck, Stourton, Farnley, Copley Hill and Neville Hill) were to give excellent service for approximately one hundred years before meeting their end with the demise of steam power in the 1960s. Holbeck survived as a fuelling and servicing point and Neville Hill, which was the last to be opened as late as 1904 became a diesel depot in June 1966. After being completely modernised, it became in 1978 a service shed for the Inter-City 125 high speed trains and local diesel services, including servicing facilities for diesel units, coaches and carriage cleaning. Again, on the very first day of revenue earning service, between Leeds and London King's Cross, 2nd October 1989, the InterCity 225 electric service with class 91 locomotive would be serviced at Neville Hill.

From the late 1980s to 1993 British Rail often made a profit, something a nationalised railway industry anywhere in the world rarely did but the political situation was such that each time it made a profit, the government of the day promptly cut the subsidy. There had been some major achievements and one of the most important as far as Leeds was concerned, was the decision to proceed with electrification of the East Coast Main Line. The £500 million, seven-year scheme was to make the route the longest building site in the world. It involved 157 bridges being rebuilt or demolished, the erection of over 29,000 masts, 1,400 miles of overhead electric wire, 14 feeder stations from the national grid and three power control centres. Included in the scheme were new signalling schemes for the York and Newcastle areas, which were officially opened on 14th May 1990, and 16th April 1992 respectively. Being too technical to be known as mere signal-boxes, they were now called 'Integrated Electronic Control Centres' (IECCs).

On the 15th May 1989 after many months of trials and training of staff, particularly, Leeds train crews, the new Class 91 electric locomotive of the InterCity 225 made the inaugural run from Leeds to London King's Cross albeit hauling older Mark 3 coaches. The inaugural run of an InterCity 225 train between Leeds and King's Cross with new Mark 4 coaches took place on the 20th September 1989, the regular service commencing on the Leeds part of the route on 2nd October 1989. In 1993 the government announced that the railway industry was to be privatised and soon there was a scramble by interested companies for parts of the railway system, which in a few short years changed out of all recognition. It is a matter of opinion as to if it was for the better, but among old and present railwaymen there is much divided opinion.

Railtrack, the new owners of Leeds Station, soon realised that it was managing far more trains and passengers than it was ever designed for. Leeds Station is built on a maze of vaulted structures known as the 'Dark Arches'. 455 vaulted arches support the station over two main roads, the River Aire and the Leeds-Liverpool Canal. The station environment was poor and reliability and punctuality of

23

services was deteriorating. Sweeping changes were essential to meet present-day requirements and to bring the station and infrastructure up to standard to meet the challenge of the new century. Work began in October 1999 on the £245 million ambitious transformation of the station and infrastructure. By far the largest part of the investment was spent on improving track, signalling, overhead line electrification equipment and related works.

Two new tracks were constructed at the west end of Leeds Station giving a 50% increase in track capacity and bringing to an end years of congestion and delays at this well-known bottleneck. This west end 'throat' area, where 80% of all trains to and from Leeds arrive and depart, could now deal with 40 trains an hour in each direction and each major rail corridor to and from the west had an almost dedicated route into the station. The layout within the station was extensively remodelled to provide greater operational flexibility. New signalling completely replaced the virtually 40-year-old former system, with 140 new signals and 15 new gantries. All the signals were fitted with the Train Protection and Warning system (TPWS) and the signalling operations, formerly controlled by Leeds Power Box, were transferred to the specially extended Integrated Electronic Control Centre (IECC) at York. The equipment supporting the electrical overhead wires was designed so that each of the western approach lines was independently wired and, should a fault occur, only the section directly affected needed to be isolated. Major bridge works were carried out to reconstruct Globe Road, Whitehall Road, Gelderd Road (two bridges over the duel carriageway), Swinegate and Holbeck.

Leeds Station could now boast an impressive seventeen platforms. In 1998 an old parcels platform (the last surviving platform of the old Leeds City North Station) was refurbished to meet the increased demand for platform space. Initially it was known as platform W now it is platform 1. In addition four new platforms were constructed to improve capacity for trains and passengers. All the original platforms were reconstructed and some extended. The station was given a brand new roof, much higher than the one it replaced with an integral lighting system and extensive glazing. The former North Concourse, long used as a car park, was transformed to its 1930s former glory, bustling with shops and cafes. A new glazed footbridge with six escalators, stairways and five passenger operated lifts replaced the old subway, improving access for the passengers. Together with new toilets, waiting rooms and shelters, a new customer information and public address system were installed covering the whole of the station. The whole project was completed on the 31st May 2002 finally bringing to Leeds a station that befitted its status as a major city and economic centre.

STEAM

The engine driver in the heyday of steam was the modern equivalent of today's astronaut. Until the demise of steam engines in the mid 1960s it was nearly every schoolboy's dream to be an engine driver. The chance to be in charge of an enormous piece of living machinery which had the awesome power to transport hundreds of passengers, at speeds in excess of 70 miles per hour. It provoked the industrial revolution and provided the masses with the means of travelling the country, never imagined before. Some of these steam engines were to become more famous than film stars and certainly outlasted them. Today, some forty years on, railway museums and private steam railways are a major tourist attraction for young and old alike, such is the public's fascination and love affair with the mighty steam engine. There was always a glamour attached to these monsters and an excitement when even adults were making a train journey.

A lasting memory I treasure of a freight train called '*The Bull*' departing from Normanton South Yard every weekday for the journey to Sheffield. It really did remind me of a bull as, from a standing start, it hissed, snorted and growled its way out of the yard, with fire, ashes, smoke and steam belching skywards, as it struggled with its heavy load. By the time it reached my signal box (Goose Hill Junction) the driver by using all his skills and experience would be beaming all over his face as the train picked up speed and was able to pull the heavy load with less effort. In reality, being an engine driver or fireman was far removed from the glamour often projected. Who else had to serve an apprenticeship sometimes in excess of twenty years, starting as a cleaner and progressing to a fireman before obtaining the ultimate authority? Being called upon to take duty at any time of the day or night in a highly responsible task and being exposed to all the weather conditions the British climate can provide, would soon dull any sense that this was a glamorous job.

Another populous grade was the signalman. In the early days of the railways, the only form of signals, were by hand and flag signals.

These were usually carried out by special railway policemen, and in fact, signalmen to this day are still known as 'bobbies' in railway parlance: 'Hello Bobby, this is the driver of 1A24 reporting'. It was often a lonely life, unless one was fortunate enough to rise in the ranks to the bigger signal boxes, where probably two men and a boy would be on duty at any one time. In the smaller more remote boxes it could be a problem even reaching the place of work, having to walk along the trackside sometimes for many miles. Part of my signalling career was spent as a relief signalman, which meant I could be called upon to work at any one of fifteen different signal boxes. Each one of these Victorian age cabins had a special character of its own, but all had that unique pungent smell; a mixture of tobacco smoke, paraffin, floor polish, Brasso, black lead and the coal burning stove.

Why was it that some boxes were always regarded as cosy, while others were regarded as positively hostile places to work? Nearly all had the basic essentials of comfort: a paraffin Tilley lamp, situated over the train register (sheer luxury if a gas light was provided); a hard wooden locker to rest weary legs, inside which was stored a man's tea and sugar; two large enamel water cans which were replenished each day by a local goods trip working; a dry toilet situated near the signal box but only ever used in a dire emergency; a coal burning stove that served to provide both heat and the means to make a hot drink; a lamp locker to store paraffin, hand lamps and point clamps.

Some boxes were situated in beautiful countryside where in winter and summer there was an ever-changing pattern of scenery. On the night shift, watching for first light and hearing the dawn chorus erupt and seeing wild animals emerging from their slumbers, was a privilege few people have the chance to see. On a beautiful summer's day watching the platelayers working in the sun, could make one long to also work outside, but the same scene in the depths of winter, coping with hazardous conditions, would bring a realisation that one had chosen the correct job. Watching a steam train in darkness when all

27

around is covered in a blanket of snow, the train would appear, as a moving black snake in a totally contrasting environment was a sight to behold the eyes and one that I always enjoyed.

Comparing these situations with the signal box that was in a dark dank cutting or next to a tunnel could be just the opposite. Even in the height of summer some of these places never felt the sun and were always dreary and depressing places to spend a third of one's life. Often in winter, the signalman could spend his entire shift only able to see a short distance, due to the smoke and gloom that never seemed to lift. In these situations, a signalman could take duty on the night shift and never see another soul until relieved the next morning. As late as the 1950s and 60s we could have smog (fog and smoke) that could last for days on end, where the signalman's main problem was to see the tail-lamp of every train that passed. At this time, the platelayers, whom we envied working in the open in summer, we sympathised with, as they stood for hours at their appointed signals posts, to provide an audible warning to the engine drivers, as to the position of the signals.

The drivers and signalmen though were really only a small cog in an enormous machine that employed virtually every known job. I invite you, the reader, to think of a job; the odds are that the railway employed some one in that job or at least in a similar position. A sweeping statement, yes but when thought through it was almost the case. Just a few of the unusual positions that come to mind but were all employed on the railway: blacksmith, locksmith, lamplighter, stable-hand, rat-catcher, knocker-up, rent-man, upholsterer, painter, solicitor, horse-van driver, doctor, lift operator, nurse, welder, chaplain, blind-dyer, electrician, French-polisher, gas fitter, bricklayer, stonemason, boilermaker, chef, advertising, estate-agent, surveyor, architect, postman, commissionaire, lift-attendant, the list is endless. It was once said that every trade and profession was represented on the railway, except undertaking and midwifery!

THE 9.00am LEEDS TO EDINBURGH 'FLIER' IN THE YEAR 1911

This train was first put on as a daily train in the summer of 1901, leaving Leeds at 8.47am, and arriving at Edinburgh at 1.30pm. The train now departs at 9.0am and, travelling via York, covers the overall distance of 230 miles in four hours 32 minutes, an average speed of 53 miles per hour. The locomotive is a Class R, usually number 2018. The original time allowed from York to Newcastle was 90 minutes, but this was brought down to 82 minutes from 1st October 1904. In April 1910 an additional two minutes was allowed on account of slacks necessitated by pitfalls in the neighbourhood of Chester-le-Street, but still in 1911 this train is the quickest by any route from Leeds to Edinburgh.

At the present time it consists of six vehicles from Leeds to York, weighing 152 tons with accommodation for 292 passengers. Two of the vehicles are for Scarborough, and are detached at York, but an East Coast van is added and the load from York to Newcastle is 127 tons, with accommodation for 209 passengers. At Newcastle the train is increased to seven vehicles including a dining car, and the total weight is 195 tons. Having regard to all the circumstances, such for instance as the speed restrictions at Durham, Chester-le-Street, Morpeth and Berwick, and the very steep banks to be negotiated between Berwick, Grant's House and Cockburnspath, where there are several miles of 1 in 190 and 1 in 200, the performance of this train is one of the finest in the Kingdom.

Taking the 13 minutes off, allowed for attaching and detaching at York and Newcastle and allowing just one minute at each of these stations, brings the running time down to four hours 19 minutes. Nearly 100 hundred years on, the present day High Speed Train, the InterCity 125, does the same journey in three hours and four minutes, a difference of one hour and 15 minutes!

THE INTERCITY SWINGER

Ian Sykes

A 1984 photo of Supervisors Ian Sykes (standing) and Brian Whiteley

My memories of **Ian Sykes** *were of the man who used to set the London King's Cross trains off on their way from platform 5 at Leeds. A quiet man who always used to carry out his duties with due regard to the safety of his passengers and staff alike, Ian joined the service in June 1951 as a 15-year-old straight from school. He had no particular interest in the railway and the only connection was that of an uncle who was a platelayer at Hartlepool. He was sent to Low Moor No3 signal box to learn how to be a train recorder and after the initial shock and several weeks of hard training he qualified for the post. Ian found that once he got to know the ropes he actually enjoyed the work although he was not over keen on having to work shifts.*

On reaching the age of 18 years he received the call for National Service. His stationmaster had told him how to serve his time with the railway section of the Royal Engineers and after a successful interview he was eventually posted to The Royal Engineers (Railway Division) at Longmoor, Hampshire. After training, Ian passed out to be a signalman, but on the Longmoor Railway they were actually known as 'blockmen'. Whilst there a film crew came to make the epic 'Bhowani Junction' film, an adaptation of a John Masters novel. It starred Ava Gardner, Stewart Grainger and Bill Travers. Many of the soldiers were employed as extras but unfortunately at the time Ian was fully employed on signalling duties, so he never did appear on the silver screen. On returning to civilian life he passed out to be a signalman, being appointed to his first box at Wyke, near Bradford. Gaining promotion, he was to work signal boxes at Low Moor, Halifax station and Mill Lane. In 1978 Ian became station supervisor at Bradford Interchange and later carried out supervising duties at Forster Square, Halifax, Ilkley, Skipton and Keighley. In 1980 he moved to Leeds in a supervising capacity and his final move in 1984 was as regulator in the Leeds signal centre. He retired in February 2000 after 48 years service. In retirement, much of his spare time is spent with the Methodist Church.

I joined the railway not because of any interest but simply because it was a job on offer at the time. However, I was soon to catch the bug and develop a keen interest in all things railway. After serving my apprenticeship as a train recorder at 18 years of age I was required to become a National Serviceman. I joined the railway branch of the Royal Engineers. I soon qualified to become a Blockman with the army railway at Longmoor. This proved really interesting and gave me quite a bit of experience. At the time the general public could travel on the passengers trains at Longmoor free of charge on the proviso they travelled at their own risk. I was to spend the whole of my two years service at Longmoor and after demob returned to the railway, passing out to be a signalman at Wyke. After a spell there I gained promotion to Lightcliffe signal cabin, before moving on to Low Moor, which at the time was quite a busy signal box. I had an unusual experience when part of the up line suddenly disappeared down the bank side through subsidence. My next move was to Halifax station box and then my final move in the signalling grade to Mill Lane, near Bradford Interchange.

By this time (1978) many of the signal boxes were closing and the prospect for the future in signalling looked distinctly bleak. I did several courses to try and gain more experience and this eventually paid off when I was appointed supervisor at Bradford Interchange Station. I really enjoyed this work, which was vastly different from the signal box world. At first the freedom of being able to walk about was to take some getting used to. Another part of the job was dealing with the general public and of course supervising the station staff. I quite often dealt with problems quite differently from what my area manager would have done and so consequently often received his wrath.

On one Saturday night at about 11.0pm a young girl aged about 15 years came on to the station. She had purchased a single ticket to London and was sat in the waiting room. I thought it strange that a girl so young should be travelling to London on her own without any luggage and so late at night. My curiosity got the better of me and as I was worried about her I approached her and asked where she was going. She quite calmly replied 'London'. I said 'If you stay there I'll tell you when the train comes in and get you a seat near the guard, so he can keep an eye on you'. She readily agreed to my suggestion. Approximately 15 minutes later my office phone rang and a distraught woman was on the phone saying she had lost her daughter and had I seen anything of her. After giving me a brief description I was able to confirm that the young lady in question was in my waiting-room ready to travel to London. The mother arrived by taxi and persuaded her daughter to return home with her, which thankfully she did. I recorded the facts in the daily logbook. The area manager told me he would not have dealt with it in that manner. I told him that I had a daughter of a similar age and I would hope that someone would do the same for me in similar circumstances.

After a while I decided to apply for the relief supervisor's job which covered quite a few stations, one of them being Bradford Forster Square. I decided to have a look at the station before my interview. This station handled a huge amount of parcel traffic and there was a conveyor belt that covered most of the station. From this conveyor porters would unload parcel traffic and place them in cages ready for transporting. I asked the supervisor: 'What happens if the conveyor breaks down? 'Ah', he said, 'We then put plan B into operation'. At the interview I was asked the very same question by the manager, I hadn't a clue what the answer was, so I just said 'I would put plan B into operation'. The manager said 'Very good' and I got the job. I never did discover what plan B was!

Before British Rail decided to close their parcels depots the GPO at Forster Square built a huge sorting depot on the station. They invited Prince Charles to come and perform the opening ceremony. Huge crowds gathered to watch the official opening and when the Prince had departed a GPO supervisor came to me and said 'From now on, all our traffic will be coming in to Forster Square to be delivered by train'. He said 'We're going to knock some holes in the station walls so our vehicles can come straight onto the platforms and load directly into the waiting trains'. He added 'We will be providing supervisors on all three shifts to ensure smooth loading of these trains'. 'When is this due to start?' I enquired. 'Next week' was the reply. I said 'Well you won't need the supervisors at this station as the parcel depot closes next week' and it did! Bradford Forster Square was demolished after the withdrawal of parcel traffic. The site is now the new Inland Revenue Offices. The new Forster Square Station was redeveloped a quarter of a mile along the line in the direction of Shipley and provides services to and from, Leeds, Ilkley, Skipton and three services to and from London King's Cross.

On the closure of Forster Square I then moved to Leeds as supervisor. It was by far the busiest station I had ever worked at. We frequently used to have a punctuality drive, which would last for one week. The assistant station manager came to me one Monday morning and said 'It is punctuality week. I want you to ensure that every train departs on time, so be sure to ring the "train ready to start button" in good time. I want every train to leave on time'. I said I would do my best. It so happened that a certain very attractive young lady always used to travel to the capital on a particular train, which was first stop London. Invariably she would come on the station at the very last minute and being such a beautiful young lady, our gallant assistant station manager would help with her luggage, ensuring she caught the train. On this particular morning the said lady came along at the very last minute and our manager, not wanting the train delayed, grabbed her cases. After helping her into the train he followed her to stow the luggage. Following his instructions, I whistled the train out and as it started to move off, a door flew open and out jumped a red faced manager! He came up to me and said: 'You pillock! You tried to get me sent to London'. 'Sorry boss' I replied, 'I was only following your instructions'!

On night duty a rough looking man of giant proportions asked me the time of the next train to Sheffield. I informed him that he had missed it and there was nothing until the following morning. His reply was 'Well in that case I will walk along the track to Sheffield'. I told him that to attempt that would get himself killed. He walked towards the end of the platform, with my shunter colleague and myself keeping him company. He commenced walking on the track in the Sheffield direction so I immediately informed the signal box on my radio to stop the traffic in this vicinity. I also requested police assistance. We were increasingly concerned for his safety and my colleague, who was quite a big chap, tried to halt the giant's progress. This proved to be an enormous mistake as the giant literally picked him up, lifted him above his head and swung him around. I distinctly remember the shunter saying as he was propelled through the air 'I think I have bitten off more than I can chew here'! He was then unceremoniously dumped on the ground. It took the arrival of two police officers that had to wrestle him to the ground before he could be restrained and arrested for his own safety.

One Sunday evening it was my job to ensure a string of vans were attached to a parcel train bound for London King's Cross. I observed the pilot engine propel the vans onto the rear of the train and the shunter coupled them to the last vehicle. When the time of departure arrived I carried out the necessary procedures and the train departed on its way to London. The next day the boss sent for me and wanted to know why the train had travelled all the way to London without the air brake pipe connected on the vehicles we had attached. I told him that it was not my responsibility to check that procedure. Vehicles when attached to a train with the brakes inoperative are known in railway jargon as 'swingers' and ever after this incident I was known as the InterCity Swinger.

Part of my duties was supervising in the Parcels Concentration Depot (PCD). One day the railway chaplain who I knew very well came to me and said 'Would you be prepared to let six young theological students follow your parcels porters around for the week to gain experience in a working environment?' He could see that I was very worried about this prospect. I said 'You know some of these chaps are rough diamonds and your young boys could get eaten alive by them'. I also added that they must be prepared to learn new words that they had never seen in a dictionary! I said we would give it a try a day at a time to see how it goes. To my great surprise the whole exercise went off extremely well and many actually made lasting friendships. Working on the platforms every day was different and one never had the time to become bored. Working with the travelling public was an enlightening experience one that I really enjoyed and I would have no hesitation in doing it all again. In retirement, my wife and I gain immense satisfaction through our association with the Methodist Church, and the time we can now spend with our grandchildren, something we really enjoy.

THE EARLY ROADS AND CANALS

With the introduction of industrial life in the 1700s, the need to connect townships by a passable road was an essential priority. At this period most roads throughout Yorkshire were unsuitable for wheeled vehicles. Most were unsurfaced and frequently unusable except to travellers on horseback. Travellers from Leeds wishing to journey to London would go by horseback to Wakefield and join the stagecoach en route for the Great North Road. It was decided that a new system of turnpiking be tried. This followed the route of existing highways, but the turnpike system provided better administration and money for the upkeep of the roads. The principle being that users pay a toll every time they used the road. Turnpike trusts were established by an Act of Parliament, which allowed the trustees to erect gates at intervals along the roads and to employ persons to collect the tolls from travellers at a predetermined scale. In the 1740s, Leeds, Wakefield, Halifax and Doncaster were all linked to turnpike roads. The Act for the Leeds, Selby, Bradford and Halifax turnpike specifically stated that the road was for the carriage of wool, woollen manufacturers and dying. Although an improvement the turnpikes did not solve the problem of moving heavy loads over long distances; the canals were to prove better for this sort of traffic. The turnpike roads did however make possible fast stagecoach services for passengers and light mail. The heyday of the stagecoach was to last from the 1750s through to the 1840s.

Before the railways came water transport, by far the cheapest and often the faster way of moving heavy loads at the time. Initially seaport towns had a distinct advantage over inland neighbours, as they were able to import export heavy goods by ship. Some of the inland towns were able to move a limited amount of goods by river, but generally most of the Yorkshire rivers were not suitable for navigation without vast improvements. Rivers, as with roads, required an Act of Parliament and an administrative body to oversee their function. Under an Act of Parliament the Aire and Calder was placed under the control of the Proprietors of the Aire and Calder in 1699.

This enabled them to levy tolls on users of the river and to use these funds for the improvement of the river navigation. It soon became evident that building artificial waterways and linking them to existing rivers could improve the waterway transport system immensely. Yorkshire canal building commenced in the 1760s and lasted until the 1830s.

The link with Yorkshire and Lancashire was made through the Pennines by three canals. These were without doubt, some of the greatest engineering achievements of the time. The Leeds to Liverpool Canal via Skipton was open from 1796, but it would take until 1816 before through navigation all the way between Leeds and Liverpool was possible. The Rochdale Canal, which was opened in 1802, followed the Calder Valley route and the Huddersfield Narrow Canal, crossed by a tunnel under Standedge was opened in 1811. The tunnel situated between Marsden and Diggle is three miles, 171 yards long. (When the parallel rail tunnel was built later the canal was used to remove spoil, by means of horizontal adits between the two.) These Trans-Pennine canals opened up the import export of goods worldwide via the Liverpool Docks. An added bonus was to the districts through which the canals passed – enabling cheaper transport of commodities and goods. Their demise set in with the coming of the railways, duplicating all three routes during the 1840/1850 period.

IT'S ONLY ALICE

Hugh Dick

A winter scene of Hugh Dick at the controls of his Class 47 Locomotive

*Engine driver **Hugh Dick** followed his father, who was a fitter's labourer, onto the railway, starting as a 16-year-old engine cleaner at Sowerby Bridge shed on the 8th December 1941. Britain was in the depths of the Second World War and in June of 1942 Hugh was sent on loan to the big Saltley Engine shed at Birmingham. He was to spend three years in lodgings until returning to Sowerby Bridge after the war was over in June 1945. Sowerby Bridge shed was closed in January 1965 and Hugh transferred to the vast Healey Mills Freight complex. His final move was to Leeds Holbeck shed in 1965 from where he retired in 1987, having notched up 45 years' service. While at Birmingham Hugh was sent on loan to Bourneville, Redditch and Bromsgrove loco sheds and had the experience of firing 'Big Bertha' up the Lickey incline (1 in 37, some bank!). The famous 'Big Bertha' was a one-off 0-10-0 steam locomotive monster specially built to help freight and passenger trains up the Lickey Incline between Bromsgrove and Blackwell.*

On one occasion I signed on duty early morning at Saltley Shed. My driver was Jack Griffiths; his nickname was 'Honest John' and with a name like that he was evidently one of the great veteran characters of the old steam days. The engine was a Midland class, type four, the biggest locomotive allowed on the single line from Barnt Green to Stratford on Avon. We left Washwood Heath around 2.0am and arrived at Broom Junction at approximately 4.30am. John said: 'Hughie, put your feet up old lad and have a nap while I go to the signal box to see the signalman and make a pot of tea'.

Well, I put the coal pick against the boiler, leaned against it and put my feet up on the hand brake. Being a single line, we could not go until the Ashchurch parcels train had gone through to Birmingham. I soon dozed off but was brought back to reality by a tapping on my leg and a woman's voice saying: 'Have you seen him?' I flew off the engine and sprinted to the signal box to tell the signalman and Honest John I had just seen a ghost. The signalman said 'It's nothing to worry about lad, it's just old Alice' and with that he took his overcoat of the hook and went out into the night to bring Alice back to the cabin to await the police.

Apparently her husband, a platelayer, had been killed on that stretch of line some years earlier and she was often found looking for him along the line. Eventually, we set off for Stratford and on to Kineton Army Depot, where the army took over the train. It was an underground ammunition dump… I had not realised until then what sort of train we had taken. Just as well because at that time we were working trains during air raids. Anyway, after a good breakfast, free, courtesy of the Army, the soldiers handed over the locomotive and we took it back to Saltley. Needless to say, I never felt sleepy when working on the stretch of line that Alice patrolled!

The following poem was a stark reminder to Hughie and his colleagues as they delivered hundreds of tons of ammunition to the war effort, how vulnerable they were to enemy aircraft looking for the glow of an engine firebox. Hughie was working a train the night Coventry was set alight and remembers vividly the whole city on fire and more and more bombs dropping. As Hughie says, 'Nowadays they say railwaymen are facing too much stress. We were absolutely terrified every day and night we were at work'. Hugh has contributed this poem:

SIREN TIME

The sirens burst out on a sleepy town
And people withdraw to shelters down
The buzz of a plane is heard in the sky
And innocent people get ready to die

Thud! Thud! Thud! Drop the bombs with a quiver
And children in cellars start to tremble and shiver

Soon the city's aglow with buildings on fire
And for some folk out there it's their funeral pyre
Crump! Crump! Crump! Goes the sound of a gun
And so it goes on 'til the rise of the sun

And so we must pray hard for a glorious end
Therefore to God all our prayers do we send
O please, please God grant us a boon
Let the end of this havoc come very soon.

THE JOYS OF THE EARLY TRAVELLER

It took the Regulation of Railways Act 1844 to force reluctant railways to put roofs on third-class carriages. It also stipulated that at least one third class service per day be run to all stations; these being known as Parliamentary trains. Before 1870 a railway journey whether in covered carriages or open was always very basic. There were no corridor trains, very poor lighting, virtually no heating, toilets nor refreshment cars, and sleeping facilities were unheard of. Lighting was by oil lamps that were very temperamental on moving trains and prone to many problems. The first form of heating was when the Great Northern Railway introduced flat metal foot-warmers filled with boiling water from special foot-warmer huts positioned along the route. It was not until the early 1900s that steam heating from the train engine was gradually introduced.

The first sleeping cars, for first class passengers only, were produced by the North British Railway for the East Coast Route on the 31st July 1873. The London & North Western followed on the 1st October of the same year. It was a long time before the railway companies realised that third class passengers also required sleep and it was the Great Western who first provided the facility as late as 1928. In 1879 the Great Northern Railway introduced the first dining cars but, because there were no corridors, passengers had to pay an extra two shillings and six-pence (12½ pence) for the privilege of sitting in the dining carriage. Restaurant cars gradually came into general use in the early 1880s. The fitting of bogie wheels at each end of a carriage enabled much longer vehicles with a bigger passenger-carrying capacity to be produced. They filtered into the country in the 1870s but were not in widespread use until a quarter of a century later.

Going to the toilet was always a problem for the early rail traveller. Many devices were produced so that the desperate passenger could relieve him- or herself. But how to get any privacy to carry out this function in a crowded carriage with no corridor was another matter?

Again the Great Western came to the rescue when in 1892 they commenced putting corridors on long distance trains and giving the guard a key to allow passengers to use the toilet situated at the end of the carriage. It took the Regulation of Railways Act 1868 for the first communication cord to be introduced on all trains travelling 20 miles and over. The cord was situated below the gutter, on the outside of the train. The internal communication cord that gradually applied the brake was introduced from about 1899. So, next time you want a moan when making a rail journey; spare a thought for our Victorian ancestors!

WHAT DO YOU KNOW ABOUT ELEPHANTS?

David Eyers

A recent picture of David Eyers giving his pride and joy some T.L.C.

*The word 'gentleman' is not one that should be used lightly, but when talking about **David Eyers** the word is truly appropriate. I have known him in his capacity as a ticket inspector and trains inspector for many years. I worked with him on many occasions, sometimes in very difficult situations, and his manner in dealing with people was always impeccable. True, when dealing with the odd objectionable customer, he could often come out with a one liner, to put that person in his place, but even then he did it in a nice manner.*

David was just 17 years old when he volunteered for the army in 1946. He joined the 1ˢᵗ Royal Dragoon Guards simply because he knew they had Daimler armoured cars, which he was fascinated with. Most of his time was spent in Germany and he soon made a point of learning the language - it was easier to chat the fräuleins up! It was to stand him in good stead for he met and married a young German girl and was to have a long and happy marriage, until unfortunately she passed away just recently.

He had no immediate family connections with the railway but after six years' Army service he joined the railway as a porter at London King's Cross on the 2ⁿᵈ December 1952. He was to stay in this post for six years until he gained promotion to a passenger guard. He gained a wealth of experience and after 16 years was promoted to a travelling ticket inspector; a post he held for 17 years. His final position was senior trains inspector from which post he retired in 1994 having completed 41 years service, all of it based at King's Cross. He did however, throughout his career, often work at Leeds in his capacity of guard, ticket inspector and trains inspector so he is well qualified to make a contribution to this book. In retirement, his hobbies are solving cross words and setting them for a country magazine, and a special interest in the opera.

During my service with the 1st Royal Dragoon Guards we had perhaps two claims to fame. Our commanding officer in Germany, who had lost a leg during the war, was Colonel Heathcote-Amory, whose brother was the Tory Chancellor of the Exchequer. I have a somewhat remarkable story concerning the next claim. For most of my career, in order to gain promotion, I took charge of the medical centre under various medical officers. When the regiment completed its duties in Germany I was almost due for demob. However, because of the Korean War I had an extra year added to my service. This meant I had to join the Royals in Egypt after a spell in Chester Hospital to complete my six years service. At that stage I was a full Corporal in charge of the medical centre again. To my complete and utter amazement we were joined by a Lieutenant Robert Fleming, RAMC, whose father was the world famous Sir Alexander Fleming, the Scottish bacteriologist who discovered Penicillin.

Sick parade was held first thing in the morning. There were no medical secrets in the army. I would sit at my desk in the consulting room with the medical officer who would prescribe treatment on a slip of paper, which I would then give to an orderly in the medical room. During Robert Fleming's first sick parade, a trooper came in to see him with a very nasty rash. The doctor looked at him and said: 'Good Lord young man, what on earth have you got there?' The reply was obvious: 'I thought you could tell me sir'. Robert looked at me and said: 'Have you ever seen anything like this Corporal Eyers?'

Obviously due to my own experience in a very hot climate I had to suggest it was 'Prickly Heat'. He said: 'So that's Prickly Heat' then rather sheepishly after a pause, 'What is the treatment for this condition?' I suggested dabbing it with Calamine lotion. Later it dawned on me, here was the son of a famous professor asking David Eyers to identify a disease and recommend its treatment, it's a funny old world.

Some forty years ago as a passenger guard I was working a summer relief train to Scotland and I was to be relieved at York. In those days we did not examine tickets but we did patrol the train to ensure everything was in order. Making my way through the train I was accosted by a very angry woman. Apparently she had booked a seat but it had not been reserved, although she had found another. Furthermore, she had expected to find a buffet car, which was non-existent. This was run of the mill stuff for a guard to deal with. Offer apologies and explain we seldom had sufficient buffet cars to cover relief trains or the staff to run them, and tell her that the complaint would be forwarded to the appropriate authorities. To my surprise she said, 'Oh don't bother, I've already had my own back on British Rail'. I was horrified. I had visions of a fire extinguisher being hurled from the train or a toilet being smashed up. I blurted out 'Madam, I hesitate to ask what you have done, but are you going to own up?' She smiled serenely and very proudly said; 'I only have a second class ticket, but I have just had a diddle in a first class toilet'. Those were her exact words. We both had a good giggle.

One of the strangest incidents took place many years ago when I was a passenger guard. A few of the guards at King's Cross were familiar with the route from our station to Clapham Junction. We guards worked what was known as passenger rated goods traffic. This junction the busiest in the world, making it necessary to arrange trips, either on a Sunday afternoon or during the night. The goods roads are sited in the centre of the complex there, which meant that once in the sidings it is difficult for the signalman to find a path onto the running lines. One night I travelled with an engine and brake to pick up some vans and bring them back to our suburban station. On arrival I reported to the yardmaster. The sort of traffic conveyed was an assortment of mostly perishable goods, livestock and on occasion a corpse. I found my vans, which I had to examine very carefully because the Southern Region was electrified with the third rail system. During this procedure I noticed a large van, which gave me cause for concern. Our return journey for part of the way would be over the oldest underground system in the world; namely the Metropolitan line built originally in 1865 from Paddington to Farringdon. A spur from this line was a rising gradient through a tunnel with a restricted loading gauge, one fork leading to St Pancras, and the other to our station, King's Cross.

I enquired at the office if anyone knew the loading gauge for the tunnel through which we would pass. My concern centred on the size of the van. The inspector in charge looked at me disdainfully and said: 'You've got a bigger problem than you thought then'. On querying this remark, he informed me that the van contained three fully-grown elephants with their calves. I did not gather the importance of this remark and felt that if someone was taking the mickey, I can be somewhat disrespectful myself. I said 'Are you suggesting I must walk them through the tunnel then?' He said 'What do you know about elephants?' I replied: 'As much as you know about the duck-billed platypus!' The situation was extraordinary. Here I was at 3.0am in the morning at Clapham Junction getting a lesson in wildlife. It appears that these huge pachyderms have more interesting habits that taking buns from a child's hand. They constantly transfer their weight from one leg to another. In a railway van of course this sets up an oscillation, which causes the vehicle to swing from side to side on its suspension. I had visions of soot being scrapped off the wall as we went though. Fortunately, we came to no arm, but it was one of the worst journeys I have ever undertaken.

Covering a higher-grade job I made my way to Biggleswade Station in Bedfordshire to join a train that had commenced its journey at Peterborough. The train was next stop London and it was full of commuters. On arrival, it stopped short in the platform, leaving the last coach unavailable for the overcrowded passengers. On boarding the train the internal intermediate door to this coach was locked. I used my key to unlock it and the passengers were very grateful and thanked me profusely. During the journey I checked passengers tickets and eventually arrived at the front of the train where the guard was sitting in his van reading a newspaper. I said, 'Do you realise that passengers are standing and yet one of your coaches was locked out of use and if I had not got on the train there would be a lot more standing?' He said, 'You have not unlocked that door have you?' 'I certainly have' I replied. 'Then on your head be it' he said. 'That coach is full of fleas, and there was not time to label it'. 'It is being taken to Bounds Green to be fumigated'. Neither of us had the guts to tell the passengers!

During my time as a ticket inspector one incident stood out when I deliberately conned a member of the public. We had recently been issued with hand-held organisers, which were downloaded with numbers of stolen tickets, ostensibly to catch out these fraudsters. I soon found another use for them. I would use every spare minute to put train fares into its memory, so saving me carrying a bulky fares manual through the train. The result of this was many of the fares soon got stuck in my own memory, including the discounted fares with the various railcards. On one occasion I was working on a packed train when a student requested a ticket to Bradford. Unfortunately, some of these people tend to look down on railway staff, and it soon became apparent he fitted this description. I asked him to put his railcard away as discounts were not available on trains, only at booking offices. He became very angry and fired several questions at me concerning fares. He would quote a ticket, single, return, saver or supersaver and ask the price the public would have to pay and then how much it would be should his railcard be available for the 34% discount. I knew the answer to these questions of course by memory, but each time he fired a query at me I waited a few seconds before giving the fare, as if I was calculating it in my head. Passengers sitting nearby were visibly impressed and the student was becoming more and more deflated. It was if some latter day Albert Einstein was checking tickets. I did this to convey to the student that he was not some superior being but that there were ordinary working people who could put him in his place.

My knowledge of the German language once came in very handy when working a northbound train with a Leeds senior conductor. The train carried certain ticket restrictions and the senior conductor told me he had a problem with a party of fifteen German businessmen who held invalid tickets. I suggested to him: 'Why don't you speak to them in their own language? He said: 'If you are so clever why don't you?' I have to admit, I was showing off a bit when I approached the party and said; 'Guten abend meine Herrschaften, es ist mir gesagt worden Sie haben Probleme mit Ihren fahrkarten'. As near as dammit it translates as: 'Good evening gentlemen, I have been informed you have problems with your travel tickets'. The senior conductor was gobsmacked. I had to jog his memory to calculate the excess fare owing, multiplied by fifteen and issue a receipt. The senior conductor was now a happy man, as he had just earned commission on fifteen excess fares.

This story belongs to George Case, who was for many years assistant station manager at King's Cross. The late Princess Margaret was to make a trip by train from King's Cross to Scotland. George had the responsibility of ensuring everything ran smoothly. A first class compartment was reserved for herself and party. The platform had been swept several times and the platform edge whitened. Royal guests usually approached the train from a side entrance to avoid the general public and the transport police had put tape barriers in place. Shortly before her arrival George decided to make a final check. He took with him a young porter who was a kind of general dogsbody. They approached the train to find many passengers had got wind of the royal visit and were waiting patiently for her arrival behind the barriers. To George's surprise a woman had got past the police cordon and was walking her dog down the platform. No harm was done until suddenly the dog squat down and had a bowel movement right in the area where the royal guest would join the train.

Naturally, George was beside himself and muttered some very choice words to his young companion. Had this mess been somewhat old, it would have been quite easy to move it along with a shoe and tip it over the platform edge. However, this was quite a different problem. The heap had just been deposited; it was still warm with a few wisps of steam rising from it. George suggested it could only happen to him, whereupon to his horror, in full view of the police and the waiting crowds, the young man said, 'Leave it to me Mr Case'. He bent down and with his bare hand scooped up as much as he could and put it in his trouser pocket. With a few deft movements of his foot, he spread what was left thinly on the ground. He had saved the day! Princess Margaret arrived unaware of the dirty deed that had just been performed. It is pertinent to point out, because of the young man's lowly status on the station that he was not called upon to shake hands with the royal guest!

There was a sequel to the story. Some weeks later George invited the young helper to his office for a cup of tea and a biscuit as a reward for his valiant effort on the day of the royal visit. The lad said his mother had taken his uniform to the cleaners and when she collected it there was a note attached to the trousers. This suggested that in future would she please check the pockets before handing them in, as they had found five ounces of snuff in one of the trouser pockets!

COMMERCIAL BREAKS

Booking Office: Provided for the use of passengers to purchase rail tickets. The term as survived from the days of the stagecoach when all transactions were entered into a book.

Edmondson Ticket: The cardboard railway ticket invented by Thomas Edmondson (1752-1851), a station master, and was used on British railways for nearly 150 years. 2¼ ins long by 1¼ ins wide this type of ticket was used by every major railway operating company throughout the industrialised world.

1835: First, second and third class of travel available from most railway companies.

1844: The Regulation of Railways Act: Beginning of Parliamentary class of travel, to provide at least one train per day and to include seats and a roof over passenger's head.

1870: Three quarters of all rail travel in Britain is by third class.

1889: Regulation of Railways Act, requires that fares be shown on all ordinary single and return tickets.

1893: Introduction of the railway platform ticket.

1906: Automatic ticket machines established at Farringdon Street on the Metropolitan Railway.

1924: Members of Parliament allowed free passes for railway travel.

1939: World War II. Special issue of ticket produced for Evacuees.

1946: Rail fares increased by 55% over pre-war levels.

1956: British Railways renames third class 'second class'.

1970: Introduction of the 'National Cash Register 21' (NCR21) ticket.

1971: Decimalisation of the British currency.

1975: Introduction of first Senior Citizen Railcards.

1979: Family Railcard made available.

1986: All Purpose Ticket Issuing System (APTIS) introduced.

1986: Portable Ticket Issue System (PORTIS) introduced.

1994: Tribute: Joint Venture Company. Ticket issuing system.

A LIVING NIGHTMARE

Bob Oliver

'Ledsham Station' (Wirral) 1957 - young station master, Bob Oliver
flanked by porters, Stewart Roberts and Ken Keene

I first became aware of **Bob Oliver** *during the time we both worked
at Leeds. Although he was the Area Manager I worked for the
Divisional Manager's Office based in Aire Street, Leeds. As a result,
I did not come under his authority and in actual fact had very little
to do with him, apart from an occasional passing the time of day.
The thing I did however notice about the man was his turnout, not
just the normal appearance one would expect from a person in his
position; but from head to foot he was always immaculate. His
personal grooming was always impeccable, his suits were always
clean and well looked after, the trousers always had a sharp crease
and his footwear always highly polished. These are attributes I
like to see in a person, although for most railwaymen, due to the
nature of their duties, it was impossible to achieve. So, in my opinion,
he always set a good example for the rest of his organisation to
follow.*

*Leaving school at Waterloo, Liverpool, just 14 years old, his first
job was as an apprentice plumber. When seventeen and a half he
volunteered for the Royal Navy as a writer (ship's clerk) seeing
service in the 'far east' on the County class cruiser H.M.S.
Devonshire. On returning to civilian life Bob thought he would*

follow in his brother's footsteps by joining the railway. His first appointment was as a booking clerk at Marsh Lane Station (between Liverpool and Southport). In late 1952 he achieved his ambition by becoming stationmaster at Halebank station. By 1961 he was relief stationmaster at Rugby. In 1962 he was appointed Assistant Station Master at Chester following which he had a spell in Bangor. In 1965 he became Station Manager at Blackburn and two years later moved on to be Area Manager, Preston. His appointment to Area Manager Leeds came in January 1970, the position he held until taking early retirement in May 1983.

Bob immediately took his talents to the North Yorkshire Moors Railway as Line Manager in a full-time capacity for just over one year. All his life his hobby has been bee keeping, from which he has obtained a vast amount of pleasure and at times, as the reader will discover, some considerable embarrassment. For a 10-year period after retirement he was Bee Diseases Officer for the Ministry of Agriculture, Food and Fisheries, covering Lancashire, Greater Manchester, Merseyside and the Wirral. His other hobby, which he still pursues, is making his own furniture. Bob is president of the Leeds Retired Staff Association.

It was a lovely September day. The sun was beginning its descent in the sky as my car travelled along the A41 road to Chester. Earlier in the day, Monday to be precise, I had left my home in Rugby after spending a weekend with my wife and family. I was feeling very pleased with myself, for on the 16th July, 1962, I had been appointed Assistant Station Master, Chester, and I was on my way to take up duty at 6.0pm for a 12 hours turn of work. This was a job that I had long cherished. Eighteen months previously I applied for a similar post at Holyhead, North Wales. I was one of 17 interviewees that included Harry Potts, a Relief Stationmaster at Coventry. One of the preferred requirements for the position, as shown in the vacancy list, was that a successful applicant should have knowledge of the Welsh language. When Harry was asked if he could speak Welsh, he replied 'No but I could sing you the first verse of Land of my Fathers'. He got the job, and rightly so for Harry was a very experienced and knowledgeable railway operator. Naturally I was disappointed at my lack of success, but I decided that I must broaden my experience. So when Harry's old job at Coventry was advertised I successfully applied for the post on a class-to-class transfer.

During the time I worked in that part of the Midlands, I was required to relieve all stationmasters and yard masters in the Rugby District Operating Superintendent's area. This included posts at Coventry, Nuneaton, Rugby, Northampton and Woodford Halse. At the time very extensive engineering work was being carried out on the Trent Valley lines in connection with permanent way remodelling and electrification of the West coast route between London and Manchester and Liverpool. Almost every weekend I was asked to undertake Traffic Inspector's duties monitoring the safety of District Engineer's trains as they occupied sections of track. Most of this work involved turns of 12 hours and with travelling time (by car) could result in up to 14 hours at enhanced rates of pay. This was very remunerative but the main benefit for me was the variety of operating practices that I was able to experience. My wife always made sure that I had plenty of food to sustain me throughout the day.

About 7.0am one morning I was trying to cook bacon and eggs on a small stove in the rear brake van of an engineer's train that was awaiting access to the up main line at Atherstone. The fire was very low and because the train was stationary no draught was being created. The fireman came into the van to enquire when we would be leaving. Seeing my predicament, he took me and my breakfast to his steam locomotive. After cleaning his shovel with the steam lance, he warmed it in the firebox and then placed my eggs and bacon on the shovel. Back it went into the firebox and within seconds he withdrew it again to give me a perfectly cooked meal. Probably the best breakfast I have ever tasted.

As I travelled along the road between Whitchurch and Chester in my Austin A35 car, my mind was occupied with the challenges of my new job and the problems associated with the forthcoming removal of my household effects. I was not, however, travelling alone although there were no passengers in the car with me. On top of the car roof rack, there were between 30,000 and 40,000 honeybees. The bees were enclosed in four wooden boxes (brood chambers). Each box contained eleven brood frames with a floor (closed entrance) and a top inner cover (crown board) comprising a wooden frame with two glass panels, all secured with nylon straps. These hives were the first of eight hives that I wanted to transfer from Braunston and Willoughby station to an allotment in Chester. They fitted neatly onto the roof rack, which rested on four corner rubber type suction feet. Cars of that period had a small gutter that ran each side of the roof and my rack was secured to the gutters on each side with a flat metal hook and bolt attachment that was tightened up to press the rack onto the roof. All the boxes were strapped to the roof rack with a new length of sash cord, obtained from Woolworths. I used my previous naval experience to ensure that knots would not undo and everything was tight and would not move. Outer roofs, gloves and protective veil were carried in the car boot.

The time was about 2.30pm as I passed through the hamlet of Tushingham. Although the A41 was considered a major road (the M1 had only recently opened) at this point it twisted and turned in open countryside. I remember going around one bend and seeing a Ford Zephyr car, which appeared to be moving in the same direction as myself, perhaps about 70 yards ahead. Momentarily I had a lapse of concentration, probably thinking about the amount of money I was likely to earn that week. The next thing I realised was that the Ford car was not moving, it was stationary and it was stood in the middle of the road. I could not understand why. The road at this point was quite narrow with a high hawthorn hedge on my right hand side and a similar hedge and farmhouse on the left. There was no traffic coming the other way so instinctively I turned my car to pass the Ford Zephyr to the right. It was only when I was a few feet away that I saw an open farm gate on the right hand side with the head and horns of a bull about to cross the road through the gate.

I was caught on the horns of a very real dilemma! To carry on meant a possible collision with the animal, so I applied my brakes. The result was that the front left hand mudguard of my car collided with rear right side of the Ford. My car came to an abrupt halt, but the bees did not. The roof rack, complete with all the hives, left my car with such force that the rack ended upright immediately alongside the Ford driver's door without hitting the car. I could see the driver, a middle-aged man with his wife, turn and glower at me. Intending to inspect the damage to his car and no doubt give me a piece of his mind, he opened his car door and to his very great surprise saw a cloud of insects rise to greet him. The glass crown board panels had broken and the bees escaped. He was flailing his arms around his head and giving a very good imitation of a windmill. Obviously badly stung he clambered back into his vehicle and quickly drove off. The last I ever saw of him he was driving his car in an erratic fashion away from me, as he and his wife attempted to swat the angry bees that had followed him into the car.

I was left with an immobilised car obstructing traffic in each direction, four damaged hives and thousands of bees flying around. Looking back, I should have retrieved my protective gloves and veil from the boot, but I did not. The adrenalin was racing through my body. The first thing I needed to do was to remove the boxes to the field, but my sailors knots were tight and would not release quickly. Using a knife I cut the rope and carried each box through the farm gate into the field. Imagine the scene. The two farm drovers had retreated to the far side of the field, very agitated bulls and cows were just inside the gate and I was being very badly stung. Bees were in my hair, on my face, up my shirtsleeves and trouser legs. During the many years that I have kept bees, this was the worst attack that I have experienced. As I was taking the hives to a point just inside the field, at the back of the hedge, inquisitive lorry drivers came to see the cause of the road blockage. None of them volunteered assistance and they retreated to the safety of their cabs, prepared to leave me to complete the removal of the debris.

Eventually I removed the boxes clear of the road. I don't remember how long it took but, as I was combing bees from my hair and brushing them off my clothes with my hands, a breakdown vehicle arrived. By this time a lot of the bees had relocated themselves to the hives in the field, but there were still some insects flying around my damaged car. The two men in the breakdown truck were very good for, despite the attention of some bees, they quickly hooked up the front of my Austin A35 and towed it away to their garage. The traffic started to move again just as a police car arrived with a police sergeant. After road measurements were recorded of the accident I was taken to a lay-by where I was required to give him my explanation for the collision. I had no excuse. He was a kindly police officer, for he eventually stopped a passing motorist and I was given a lift into Chester. By the time I reported for work at 6.0pm, many parts of my anatomy were swollen. The staff could not see my legs and arms, but the swelling on my hands and face were obvious and I had to tell them of the events of the day. Well, I can say that there was a lot of hilarity throughout the rest of my shift and in the days that followed I was the subject of much humour that I did not appreciate.

The sequel. On the 31st October 1962, I appeared at Broxton Magistrates Court and was fined £5 for driving without due care and attention. In addition I was ordered to pay an Advocate's fee of three guineas and my licence was endorsed. All this information, with details of the collision, was reported in the Liverpool Echo and the Chester Observer. Reporters in the court, however, were not given information about the escape of the bees; otherwise my tale might have been recorded in the national newspapers. The staff at Chester Station took delight in my notoriety and a gifted artist drew a caricature of my bees and me. But worse was to come. Because my new house in Vicars Cross, Chester, was not ready for occupation when I vacated my house in Rugby, my furniture was put into store. In such circumstances the District Traffic Superintendent's staff officer cancelled my lodging allowance of a few pounds per week. I took advantage of a furnished flat at Rock Ferry near Birkenhead and installed my family.

To get to Chester for work I used concessionary privilege tickets until a privilege season ticket was made available to me. This was against the rules and I was called to the office of the Chief Staff Clerk for interview. Mr. Roberts was a big man with a reputation as a disciplinarian. I was admonished for not seeking permission to reside temporarily in Rock Ferry and for using privilege tickets without approval. He was not sympathetic about my domestic upheaval and I had to accept his judgement. Lying on his desk was a copy of the Liverpool Echo reporting my presence in a magistrate's court and conviction for a driving offence. Because my role as assistant stationmaster was mentioned he seemed to be of the opinion that in some way I had brought adverse publicity upon the local railway scene. I was warned to avoid any further trouble with the Civil Authorities. I was furious and asked if this was a formal warning. He replied in the affirmative. Upon arrival in my temporary home that day I wrote a letter to the branch secretary of my union – The Transport Salaried Staffs Association - and complained that the Chester staff clerk had no right to criticise me for committing a driving offence in my own time. My views were quickly represented to Mr W Brownlee, the District Traffic Superintendent at Chester, and I was summoned to his office. I immediately regretted my impetuous reaction and was convinced that in future I would be a marked man and further promotion would be denied me. However, I need not have worried for Bill Brownlee laughed when I related my story and gave me a lecture that, in future, if I had any problems, I should address them to him, rather than involve my trade union. That was the end of a prolonged living nightmare.

CHESTER STATION

For a short period I was overawed by the responsibilities of the job that I had undertaken at Chester. This was a station with 14 platforms, three through lines, up and down goods lines serving a large and busy goods depot, engine shed, extensive coal sidings, carriage and wagon depot and numerous other siding lines. To the west of the station there was a triangle of lines that gave access to Birkenhead and the North Wales coast, Anglesey and Holyhead. Within the angle there were locomotive holding sidings where once engine sheds had stood. To the east of the station main lines gave access to Crewe, Warrington and Liverpool. Six signal boxes controlled all movements to, from and within these station limits. I do not know how many train movements took place within a 24 hours period, but I do recall that during the summer months all staff worked very hard to deal with a big increase in seasonal traffic. Not just with visitors to the attractive city itself, but with many holidaymakers en route to the popular resorts at Prestatyn, Rhyl, Colwyn Bay, Llandudno, Bangor and many other beautiful parts of North Wales. In 1962 the majority of people still enjoyed their holidays in Britain rather than the Costa Brava. In addition there were about 11 passenger services in each direction to and from Holyhead and other stations in England, many of them serving the Sealink vessels that plied between Holyhead and Dun Laoghaire.

Mr. Thompson was the stationmaster when I first assumed my duties at Chester. At various times during the day he would walk around the platforms conspicuous in his frock coat and hat, seemingly to assure himself that his staff was doing their jobs. He was an austere and remote man and you did not pass the time of day with him unless he spoke to you first. Each of the assistants did, however, have direct access to him if there was any operational problem that required his guidance or attention. I cannot recall that he ever intervened in any problem on my shift. The Assistant Station Managers (A.S.Ms), of which I was one, were graded class 1. There were two class two inspectors (early and late shifts), two class three inspectors (early and late shifts) and three class three inspectors (early, late and night shifts). The class three inspector on my turn of duty was Tom Pope, a local man who had gained promotion through the shunting grades.

At first Tom regarded me with apprehension. I suppose he did not quite know what to expect from a young man 20 years his junior. Appointments to the grades of assistant station or yard masters usually came from very experienced railwaymen who could demonstrate wide experience in and knowledge of operating practices, or management trainees who would be given the opportunity to demonstrate their potential and management skills at the sharp end of passenger and freight train operations. I did not fit into either category. We developed a good working relationship and Tom gave me a lot of help in dealing with many problems that occurred during my time at Chester. I cannot remember the total staff complement, but we supervised all the platform staff, passenger and freight shunters and liaised with drivers, guards, signalmen and staff in the Chester Control office.

On taking charge my first objective was to familiarise myself with the passenger timetable. It was made clear to me by Mr Thompson that I was to be seen by staff and public at as many main line and commuter services as possible. Naturally, passengers were always seeking information and assurances about the availability and platform location of train services that interested them. My smart uniform and gold braided peak cap was often a beacon for passengers unsure about their train service and it must have been disconcerting for some people to realise that the man they were consulting was not so sure himself. Eventually, however, my knowledge became complete and I dispensed information with confidence.

The first occasion that I was in charge on a late turn of duty, Tom advised me that it was traditional and expected that the A.S.M. would be in attendance to the 5.40pm London Euston to Holyhead *Emerald Isle* due in Chester at 9.19pm, platform 5, to supervise the splitting of the train into three portions. The first portion was to depart to Holyhead, the second portion to Llandudno and the remaining carriages would be destined for Birkenhead. The procedure was that after the train had come to a stand and passengers had detrained and entrained, a passenger shunter would split the first portion (four coaches), reconnect the vacuum and steam pipes, affix a tail lamp and the Holyhead section could then depart. A locomotive would set back onto the Llandudno coaches; they would be similarly dealt with and, after departing, another locomotive would arrive onto the remaining section destined for Birkenhead.

These procedures involved supervision of shunters, loco men and guards and were controlled by the A.S.M. using his oil fuelled hand lamp to give signals to the respective staff.

The departure of each train was preceded by the A.S.M. giving a white hand signal held head height to the guard indicating that platform duties were complete. The guard in turn would give a green hand signal to the driver for the train to depart. I assured Tom that I was competent to supervise the work and the first night everything went smoothly, all sections departing on time. On the second evening I was waiting for the fireman of the Birkenhead locomotive to couple his steam engine to the train, when a man under the influence of drink pestered me to give him a light for his cigarette. I told him I had not got any matches but he kept saying 'gizza a light mate, gizza a light from your lamp.' I turned towards the rear of the train and the man wanting a light; opened the lens of my hand lamp and offered him the naked flame. The guard saw the white light, took it as platform duties completed and without checking his vacuum brake gauge gave the green light signal for the train to depart. Panic! The fireman was still on the track at the rear of his engine, and the driver had not released the vacuum brake. No harm done, but I got a rollicking from the driver. Thereafter I made sure that no one was allowed to distract my attention when involved with similar operating practices.

The train side work was not just concerned with passengers. Almost every passenger train conveyed parcels, post office letter mail and parcels post and all these consignments had to be unloaded within the station allowance time. Designated parcels porters assisted the platform porters and they worked very quickly to complete their tasks without incurring delay to the train. A guard's van often contained livestock of all kinds: dogs, cats, fowl, exotic birds, honey bees, etc. These were packed in various crates or containers that did not always keep their occupants enclosed and safe. It was not unusual for a coffin to be carried on the floor of the van. But in addition trains frequently conveyed an extra vehicle to be detached from the rear. Horseboxes, complete loads of parcels for one-consignee and bullion vans. As the name suggests the latter vehicles contained large amounts of cash destined for banks in the area and great secrecy surrounded such consignments, with staff advised only on a need-to-know basis. The coaching stock diagrams also provided for the regular movement of empty coaches and these had to be detached. All such vehicles were removed by the station pilot engine.

This was still the age of the steam locomotive, although English Electric Type 4s were in use on a few trains including the *Irish Mail*. In 1962 Castle and Hall class steam locomotives were still hauling the G.W.R. services from London Paddington, via Shrewsbury to Birkenhead Woodside, and they made a great sight as they coasted round the southern leg of the triangle before coming to a stand in the up and down platform line. The most common locomotives were the Black Fives. Diesel Multiple Units were not used in the Chester area until 1963.

I did not particularly like working night shift, I could not get used to going to bed during the daylight hours. But of the three turns of duty it was the workload that I liked best; there were fewer passengers about, it was more relaxed and the variety of tasks made it more interesting. Once the late night local passenger trains had departed, parcel services became the priority. During the day vans were stabled and loaded in a number of bay platforms, mainly in the Whitchurch Wing. Parcels and parcels post were loaded in accordance with marshalling and loading orders. Every parcel had a sort code and consignments were loaded into vans and van sections according to destination. When a parcel train arrived in platform 5, groups of porters would enter vans throughout the train, knowing just where Chester and Chester transfer traffic was located. Other porters would load originating traffic into the required sections for onward transit. For a time there would be frantic activity until the work was completed and the onward service departed, hopefully to schedule.

There was an originating parcel train made up with vehicles from Chester and other stations. This was the 12.50am Chester to Bangor.

It was a Class C train; vacuum braked and steam heated throughout. The January night was cold. A few minutes before the train was due to depart the guard informed me that it was not complete: it was in two sections, closed up but not coupled. The shunters had not done their job properly and when I called for one of them to attend I was rebuffed – they were having a meal break. I had had an argument with the Yard Foreman (shunter) earlier in the shift over work schedules, he was Chairman of the Station Local Departmental Committee and it appeared to be his way of making things awkward for me. The guard refused to undertake the coupling work, the train was already late, so I dropped onto the track between the vehicles. Connecting the vehicles with the screw coupling was easy enough; joining the vacuum pipes took a little longer, a certain knack is required. But I could not engage the steam pipes. Station Foreman Bob Jones appeared above me on the platform: 'Get out of there Boss' he said 'That's no place for you'. I dutifully obeyed and watched as he completed the job. I was grateful for his support and thanked him. Like Tom he was a loyal colleague.

When there were no trains requiring attention the station would become eerily quiet, no porters to be seen anywhere unless cleaning and other domestic duties were being performed. I soon became aware that in between periods of work activity the platform and parcels porters found refuge in empty carriages stabled in platform 6, adjacent to the down platform where most of the night's work was performed. As soon as a train came in they were aroused from slumber and work recommenced. Shortly after 1.30am the Manchester News parcels train arrived in platform 5. Staff descended on the train and newspapers, parcels and fish boxes were promptly unloaded. A section of the staff was designated fish porters and their clothes were impregnated with the smell of fish. They stunk to high heaven. The fish vans were usually unlit 4-wheeled vehicles, but the porters seemed to know instinctively where the Chester traffic was. The boxes contained fish and crushed ice and they were usually pulled to the door of each van with a type of hook similar to a docker's hook used on bales of cotton. The floors of the vans were slippy and profane language would sometimes be heard as a man lost his footing.

Before the arrival of this train employees of newspaper distributors would assemble trestle tables on the concourse between platform 5 and the main station buildings. As soon as newspapers were unloaded they were stacked beside the dozen or so tables and without reference to any order lists, bundles of newspapers were made up for every newsagent in the city and surrounding areas. In addition consignments were packed and labelled for onward transit by road and rail to more distant places in Cheshire and North Wales. The speed at which the men worked amazed me; time was of the essence, for most of the work was completed in an hour. For such assistance as we gave, railway staff were rewarded with copies of the daily editions. Every night I was given an armful of newspapers of every type for distribution to my fellow A.S.M.s, the Control Office and of course, the District Traffic Superintendent. During my time at Chester I never had to buy a newspaper.

At the south and of the station, adjacent to the 'Whitchurch Wing' there was a small group of sidings known as 'Flanders', one of these siding lines was also called 'Vimy Ridge', connotations of the Great War. Local vagrants used the empty carriages stabled there, as a 'doss house'. One such tramp was known to the staff as 'Ambrosia', because every night he would consume a tin of rice pudding on a seat outside the station. The empty coaches were sometimes also used for the same purpose by R.A.F. personnel returning from leave to their base at Valley air base, on Anglesey. This usually occurred when they had missed the last evening connection. One night about 12.30am the Parcels Foreman suggested that I take a look in the porters room. Upon opening the door there were sounds of merriment and a shout of 'Off. Off'. There standing on a wooden table was an inebriated young member of the Women's Auxiliary Air Force unbuttoning her blouse. She had already discarded her blue jacket. Trying not to smirk, I ordered her out of the room in my most officious voice. Meekly she obeyed and I left the room with the sound of boos ringing in my ears. I was not very popular that night.

Between 1.0am and 3.30am there were two down trains to Holyhead and three up trains from Holyhead, all to be dealt with in between periods of parcel trains activities. But not only passengers were conveyed from Holyhead, for the boats from Eire also carried large numbers of cattle. The animals were loaded into wagons specially designed for the purpose and long trains made up for despatch to three or four destinations in England. These trains were routed over the up goods line, adjacent to the middle yard and the main goods depot. Part of the A.S.M's responsibilities included supervision of three-yard inspectors and freight shunting staff. They were very efficient and rarely required assistance, but I was sometimes called to monitor and record details of cattle trains being stopped to enable cattle that had lost their footing and required assistance or veterinary help. It was not a pleasant job for those who had to enter the wagons when they were shunted to a cattle dock. I must admit that I kept my distance and left other more experienced staff to deal with the unfortunate animals.

I look back on my time as A.S.M. at Chester with a great deal of nostalgia. It was a very valuable learning curve for me at a time when the railways were still very busy with freight, parcels and passenger traffic. A time when most trains were still steam hauled, and a time just before proposals made by Dr Beeching became effective. Most of the railway personnel were people of fairly long service and very experienced, their intricate knowledge of operating and terminal work contributed to the efficient implementation and operation of the Freight and Passenger Working Time Tables. They were a very good team, managed I must say by one of the best professional railway managers I have ever worked with - Mr Ken Winterton took over the post of Station Master when Mr. Thompson retired in 1963.

On the 3rd February 1964, I left my job at Chester to take up a totally different role as Freight Sales Representative for all of North Wales, located Bangor. This was one of a number of new posts created by a man seconded from outside industry and given a job as Regional Commercial Manager by Dr Beeching. So began another extremely interesting and totally different facet of my railway experience. But that is another story.

65

This little tale is rather rude
But do not take it lightly,
It's all about a female nude
And Supervisor Brightley.

A comely damsel feeling bored
Decided that she'd strive,
To entertain the Railway Board
At Leeds on platform five.

Her clothes she pulled off in a flash,
The staff got all excited,
But Brian made a chivalrous dash
Their ardour he soon blighted.

From platform six he leapt across
And never did he dally,
To wrap his coat around the lass,
A modern Walter Raleigh.

What were his thoughts when he so bold
Was covering up her beauty,
'Ye'll get yer bloddy dear'th o'cold
So I must do my duty.'

The fame she sought was soon denied
And Brian can claim that he,
Tried to save a woman's pride
And preserve her chastity.

QUEEN VICTORIA

When researching railway history one begins to realise that Queen Victoria spent much of her time (between having nine children) opening new stations, hotels, bridges, viaducts etc. However she did set the seal on the railway's future when she made her first rail journey on the 13th June 1842. In anticipation of this event, the Great Western Railway Company had built a royal carriage two years previously. To mark the occasion, the engine (PHLEGETHON) hauled the special train; the driver was its designer Daniel Gooch, accompanying him on the footplate was Isambard Kingdom Brunel, two great names in railway history.

The arrival of the railways in Scotland did not please everyone. Lord Cockburn who travelled all over Scotland as a circuit judge found that people were 'mad about railways': 'The country is an asylum of railway lunatics' and expressed his thankfulness that at least he had seen Deeside before it was 'breathed over by the angel of mechanical destruction'. Although Queen Victoria enjoyed the convenience of railway travel, she would have sympathised with the old judge's hatred that compelled the traveller to be 'conveyed like parcels'. Some of her earlier journeys to her beloved Scotland were by the Royal Yacht. On the very first in 1842 an Alderney cow was on board to provide the Queen with fresh milk! Her next visit in 1844 was in the new Royal Yacht named the Victoria and Albert but the coming of the railway was soon to lessen dramatically the hazards and fatigue of the rough sea journey and the railway was soon to become her favourite mode of transport.

Many different railway companies were competing to carry her Majesty, introducing their latest technical developments, which later were incorporated for all passengers. In 1843 the Queen travelled in a royal carriage made by the London & Birmingham Railway Company, which included the first heating system, a hot water heater fed by a small boiler under the floor. It was not until 1850 that the first ever train lavatory was provided for her use, again by the G.W.R.

The London & North Western was the first to provide gas lighting in their royal carriage. The Queen promptly demanded its removal, as she much preferred oil lamps. The provision of a dining car was first introduced in 1879 but the Queen refused this facility throughout her reign, choosing to take her meals at a local hotel en route, as she once did at Normanton Station! In the year of her diamond jubilee 1897 the G.W.R. produced a brand new royal train with all the latest innovations. She was really upset when she discovered the train had electric lighting and insisted on retaining her old royal coach now over 20 years old. Yes, the railways of today have much to thank her for, but one of them is not speed, she always refused to travel at more than 40 miles per hour!

WHISKY GALORE

Brian Marshall

Signalman Brian Marshall in charge at Kirkstall Junction
24th September 1993

Brian Marshall was to follow in his grandfather's footsteps by becoming a signalman. His grandfather was for many years a signalman at Selby Swing Bridge and his uncle was a porter at Staithes, on the North Yorkshire coast. His career commenced in July 1946 after passing a medical held in an old railway coach at Manchester Victoria station. He was sent to be a train recorder at Wakefield Road signal box, on the old Midland Railway on the outskirts of Leeds. In 1947 his career was interrupted by National Service, which was spent in the Royal Air Force. He was posted to Andover, Hampshire, as an administrative clerk looking after officer cadets. He returned to the railways in 1950 and, after passing his rules examination, took over at his first signal box: Stourton Down Goods box. He then went on to work at Hunslet Lane and Rothwell Haigh before becoming a relief signalman working at any one of a dozen signal boxes. After spells at Wakefield Road, Stourton Junction and Neville Hill East Console his final move and from where he retired after 48 years signalling service was Kirkstall Junction.

My railway career started when I was a young man and out of work. I had no particular interest in the railways but a neighbour who worked in the Signal and Telegraph department said if I was interested in a job I should I should go to the Aire Street offices and ask to see the signal inspector. After passing my medical I was sent to be a train recorder (an apprentice signalman) at Wakefield Road Signal Box. The first time I entered the box I was amazed at the amount of activity that was going on. There was a man and a young boy on duty. The signalman was busy sending and receiving bell signals from a shelf above the signal frame, which contained lots of different shaped bells each of which made a different sound. Also on the shelf were block instruments, which showed the line occupation of the many different routes. From time to time the signalman would pull some of the different coloured levers over towards him and reverse others back to their original position. Suspended from the ceiling was a diagram showing the area covered by the signal box.

I was soon to learn the meaning of the different coloured levers: Red were for stop signals, yellow for caution signals, black were for points, blue for facing point locks, while white were spare levers. There were other colours but these were the main ones. The track diagram showed the area covered by the box including the location and number of all the signals and points and the relevant gradients for each route. On the rear wall of the box was an array of telephones, which from time to time made coded rings that I learned were for different signal boxes along the route. Every time the signalman sent or received messages the train recorder would make entries in the train register that was situated on a high desk in the centre rear of the box. Every so often he would use one of the telephones to report the passage of trains to the control office. My first impression was that I would never grasp what was going on, as the whole scenario seemed chaotic, yet the signalman and boy seemed perfectly happy and knew exactly what they were doing.

Eventually I passed out to be a fully qualified train recorder and I really enjoyed the work. One aspect of the job was to keep the signal box nice and clean and in many cabins this had to be achieved during the normal day's duty but at Wakefield Road we were so busy that the train recorder was booked to take duty on a Sunday morning from 8am to 4pm to carry out all the cleaning duties. This consisted of washing the brown lino floor and then polishing with Mansion Floor Polish, wash and polish the block instrument shelf; clean the lever frame and polish with Brasso all the brass lever number plates. The remainder of the day was spent attempting to clean as many of the windows both inside and out that were possible. In winter weather this was a cold and daunting job on a shaky veranda

When I was eighteen years old I was called up for National Service and sent to Bridgnorth, Shropshire, for my basic training in the Royal Air Force. After training I was posted to Andover in Hampshire for the remainder of my service. Returning from the forces I learned the Rules and Regulations and passed out to be a signalman at my first cabin; Stourton Down Goods Box. It was extremely busy as there were two shunting engines despatching wagons for any one of the many roads my signal box controlled. The shunters would shout the number of the road for each wagon or sometimes chalk the number on the buffer beam, but it sometimes resulted in confusion and a wagon going into the wrong road. The shunter would then have to send the engine into the road, attach to the wagon, draw it out and then despatch into the right road. As can be imagined this was time consuming and a lot of extra work so tempers were often frayed.

There was however perks to the job as wagonloads of whisky were often shunted from the bonded warehouse at Hunslet Lane. On one occasion one of these wagons was derailed and as a result whisky was leaking from one of the containers. Word quickly spread and railwaymen from all over the yard suddenly appeared with any container they could lay their hands on and patiently queued to fill whatever vessel they had to save the precious liquid going to waste.

When working as a relief signalman at Wortley Junction in the days of steam and the coaches were non-corridor compartment stock. We often saw young courting couples in very compromising situations particularly on the 11pm late night train from Leeds to Bradford

Forster Square. The first signalman to spot a situation developing would tell his colleague along the route what coach and compartment to look into and word would be spread along the whole route. The young couple getting into their passionate situation thinking they were totally private, unaware that a whole lot of signalmen were viewing their amorous exploits and informing their colleagues of the progress being made. It was while working in this cabin that I came to know the late Bishop Eric Treacy who at the time, approximately 1957, was the Archdeacon of Halifax. He was an ardent railway enthusiast and a renowned photographer of steam locomotives. He used to visit the box and took many pictures from this vantage point and indeed gave me a small collection of his prints.

It was while working at Kirkstall Junction signal box that I had a very tense and unnerving incident. I had accepted and cleared my signals for the high-speed train en route from Bradford Forster Square to Leeds. I had already received the train entering section signal from the box in rear, which meant the high-speed train would be hurtling by my box in four minutes' time. To this day I do not know why I did it but something seemed to tell me to walk to the north end of the signal box, which was the only location that allowed the signalman to view the walkway across all the lines. To my horror I saw two little children, a boy and a girl about six and seven years old stood in the path of the fast approaching express train. I knew it was a waste of time to reverse my signals against the train, as he would not have been able to stop in time. I ran down the steps, dashed to the crossing and gathered the two children in my arms before the train thundered by. I took the children into my box and informed the transport police who came to collect them. I never heard anything more about this incident but I do know for certain that a young man and woman are now walking about simply because something told me to walk to the far end of my signal box and look at the crossing for no particular reason.

I can honestly say I enjoyed my career on the railways and in particular the Victorian age signal boxes where I spent my working life. It was at times a lonely life and was not suited to everyone but I always got immense satisfaction and a good camaraderie with my signalling colleagues, that I still treasure in retirement.

THE EARLY VICTORIAN YEARS

In 1801, the year of the first national census, the population of Great Britain was 10,795,596, by 1851 this had rose to 20,817,000, in 1861 the figure was 23,128,000. In the early 1800s more and more people living in Britain came to earn their living from industrial work rather than from agricultural labour. At the same time the country's population increased faster than any previous time. The living conditions for the working classes in the days of railway mania were grim. Most lived a hand to mouth existence. If a worker lost his employment, which he could do at the end of a job, through illness or any one of a thousand reasons, there was nothing for him to rely on or to fall back on. Their only hope of any help was from relatives, friends, neighbours, local shops who may allow credit or the pawnbroker. Equally same for the elderly when they grew old or infirm, their only salvation was from their own children. The government did not provide unemployment allowance or give assistance in securing another job or arrange job retraining.

In manufacturing districts the rate of mortality in the working classes was appalling. Estimates for life expectancy in Leeds in the period 1820-1840 were: manufacturer 44 years, tradesman 27 years and labourer just 19 years. One of the causes of low life expectation of these people was that they were forced to live in overcrowded industrial cities. The middle and upper class could commute from the suburbs. Tuberculosis, respiratory diseases, and stomach disorders caused by living in unsanitary conditions took a heavy toll of these people. Periodic epidemics of cholera, which affected the big cities between 1820 and 1840 sliced through the working classes. The Health of the Towns Committee described the state of the streets in The Calls area of Leeds as 'more or less deficient in sewerage, unpaved, full of holes, sometimes rendered unliveable by the overflowing of sewers and drains, with ash-holes exposed to public view and never emptied'. Between May and November 1832, there were 700 deaths from cholera in Leeds alone, the majority being within a half-mile radius of Leeds Bridge.

Most of the working classes lived in near-poverty in overcrowded inadequate housing accommodation. The houses only had earth or dry closets, each one shared by several families. By the mid 1850s, gas lighting in the cities was becoming normal for the upper and middle classes. It was to take the invention of the penny slot-meter in 1890 to bring such luxury to the lower classes; prior to this they used wax, oil or tallow and, from the late 1850s, paraffin. The cooking was carried out on open fires fuelled by wood or coal. Always around the corner was the high incidence of disease, disablement and death. Yet in the main, the people who endured these conditions did not expect anything better; such resignation was in part, the product of a long history of deprivation and suffering by which, for generations past, they had become accustomed to poverty, tragedy and very limited expectations. Most were uncomplaining in their plight; they worked long and hard for very little reward. Very few concerned themselves with national events, politics or even trade union or labour movements. Their bosses or masters were from a different social society that they could never hope to penetrate.

Children had long been exploited in the labour market and even parents saw it as the norm to expect their children to contribute to the family income from as little as seven or eight years old. Many coal owners tried to enforce the 1842 Prohibition Act of children working underground, but yet they were smuggled underground to carry out simple tasks for years afterwards. In 1860 the starting age for underground coal workers was raised from ten to twelve years and it was not until the 1868 Act that prohibited anyone from employing any child under eight years old. The textile industries employed thousands of women and children and as a result the male workers were able to gain a 60-hour week by 1850. The introduction of new machinery brought its own problems to workers not used to these vast changes. The excessive noise, speed and dangerous moving parts took their toll on the workforce. In 1874 on the railway, 767 employees were killed and 2,815 were injured in the course of their duties. In the mining industry it was worse still, with an average of 1,000 workers a year being killed.

Aspirations for them were modest; the best they could hope for was to keep clear of sickness, and be able to earn a living, be respected by their fellow citizens; see their families growing up and making their way in the world and to die without debt and social sin. In the 1850s the working classes expected to be able to partake of what leisure activities were available. Enjoyable entertainment was the penny gaffs – brief shows of melodrama, the street-showman, punch & judy, peep shows, acrobatics, songsters, music and the fairground. Many public parks opened providing recreational facilities and the very popular Sunday afternoon and evening bandstand music. Very popular was the railway excursion (a first time for many), music hall, choral society, brass bands, and the emergence of football clubs, and even the theatre catered for the very poor with seating available in the pits and the gods.

Life was very different for the middle classes, as businessmen were taking to pheasant and partridge shooting as a privileged sport and it was fairly common for them to purchase or rent small shooting estates. Just a few years later they had progressed to buying or leasing grouse moors in Scotland. The LNWR were quick to spot the potential of this business and began running 'Grouse Specials' from Euston to the Highlands; the train composed of first class for the gentry and third class for the servants, domestics and workers.

In the 1870s a few of the larger railway companies began giving their workers an annual week's holiday with pay but in general holidays with pay did not come about until as late as the 1930s and it was not until after the Second World War in 1945 that they became nationally approved. The cotton workers of Lancashire were going for day trips by train to Blackpool and Southport taking advantage of the cheap excursion fares offered by the different railway companies. By 1870, Blackpool in the north and Southend in the south were regarded as the working class holiday favourites, providing many amenities and amusements. Bournemouth, Brighton and Scarborough were much more preferred by the middle classes.

Communal life was at a premium; their happiness was found in social groups such as the family, the work group, the church or chapel or, for those with a little money to spend, in the public house. The taste for beer and the public house survived all attempts to stifle it. In these places, the meaningful relationships, experiences, joys and sorrows were shared in their common cause. Life in these days was indeed very hard. At this period, Great Britain was by far the richest country in the world but anyone trying to tell the people of the industrial West Riding of Yorkshire this fact, would have had a problem trying to convince them.

THE MISSING PARCEL

Tom Hardy

A cheerful, smiling Tom Hardy

*Joining the railways in 1949 **Tom Hardy** was to give over 42 years loyal service only interrupted by serving his country as a National Serviceman in the Royal Air Force. Tom was to spend the whole of his career in the clerical grades in and around Leeds, Bradford, and Keighley, with a short spell at Sheffield. He took early retirement in 1992.*

When I reported for my first day at work on Monday 25th July 1949 to the chief clerk at Keighley Station, his first words to me were: 'Why the hell have they sent us a trainee? Don't they know its Keighley Feast Week'! He then handed me a copy of the timetable and said: 'sit down there and read that'. It was pretty hectic in the booking office that week with many excursions and enquiries and I must admit that I wasn't able to help out much.

Although I was only 15 years at the time I was expected to work all three shifts, early, late and night turn. The booking office at Keighley is on the station bridge and the clerk on night duty was isolated from the night shift inspector and two porters who were down on the platforms. This was quite a responsibility for a fifteen year old even though ticket issue was generally light. I had to check the parcels charged throughout the day and complete the daily balance. The Glasgow St Enoch to London St Pancras express called at Keighley at 2am and the London St Pancras to Glasgow St Enoch stopped at 3.15am.

I remember when the junior porter at Keighley received his notification to report to Oswestry to commence his two years National Service in the army. He asked at the enquiry office for details of a train service to get him to Oswestry at the required time. The clerk told him to get a certain train from Keighley and change at Queensbury, Halifax, Manchester, Chester and Gobowen. The young soldier-to-be was most upset because the enquiry clerk wouldn't give him the arrival and departure times for the intermediate stations, saying: 'You should have told them to give you a posting nearer home!'

The following incident happened at approximately 8.45am one Saturday morning at Bradford Forster Square Parcels Office, in the days when British Railways operated a parcels collection and delivery service. The enthusiastic junior clerk received a telephone call from a city centre shop enquiring if a particular parcel had arrived from one of their suppliers. The young lad said he would check and asked the lady if she would hold the line. He looked on the counter for the delivery sheets for that particular area but could not trace the parcel. Using his initiative he went to the station forecourt where the delivery vans were lined up. Unable to find Fred Riley, the driver for this particular round, he located his van and climbed into the back to look for the parcel.

A couple of minutes later the driver returned and promptly drove off. The lad thought about jumping out but reasoned that, as the van's first delivery was only a short distance from the station, he would wait until the driver stopped to make his first delivery. Unbeknown to the young clerk, Fred Riley had been on duty from 4.30am that morning, delivering fish to the wholesale fish market and as he was now extremely hungry had decided to nip home for some breakfast. When Fred stopped the van outside his home he was amazed to see the young clerk climb out of the back and he asked him what he thought he was playing at. The lad replied with the words 'I can't stop now, I'm on the telephone' and ran down the road to Church Bank, where he caught the first bus back to Bradford Forster Square Station and legged it back into the parcels office. Dashing to the phone, to his amazement the lady was still holding the line. He apologised for the delay and also for the fact that he hadn't been able to trace the parcel. The lady, who had been so patient, thanked him for his efforts, little realising the trouble he had really gone too. The missing parcel was delivered to the shop later that same morning!

One Christmas Eve in the early 1960s the staff in the parcels accounts office, Bradford Forster Square, and those who could be spared from the parcels office, went out at about 12.0noon to a nearby pub for a Christmas drink, as was the custom in those days. A 'fuddle' had also been organised and the sandwiches, pork pies, drinks, etc, were set out in the parcels accounts mess-room awaiting the return of the revellers. I, being the claims and correspondence clerk volunteered to remain in the office and deal with the telephone calls and any visits from members of the public, as these enquiries at the 11th hour were mainly in respect of goods, which had been ordered for Christmas but had not been delivered. Shortly after everyone had departed for the pub the stationmaster walked in, presumably to wish everyone the compliments of the season. I explained to him why I was the only one left in the office and out of courtesy asked him if he would like a drink, to which he readily signified that he would. I poured him a glass from one of the bottles and had to leave him in the mess-room as the telephone was ringing. I was kept busy answering the phones for the best part of an hour and completely forgot about our guest in the mess-room until he emerged wobbling slightly, wished me a Merry Christmas and departed.

I was still kept busy when the staff returned from the pub all ready to have a bite to eat and imbibe another glass or two. When they entered the mess-room they found more empty bottles than full ones and created an immediate uproar wanting an explanation from me as to who had drunk their Christmas Cheer. I, of course, was number one suspect and it took me some time to convince them that it wasn't me. It was fortunate that this particular stationmaster had a reputation as a drinking man or I would probably have been lynched.

GOING LOCO

Barton-Wright F15 Class: Built for the L.&Y.R. in 1857 for general freight traffic. Based at Wakefield.

Midland Johnson Class: Introduced in 1875. Nearly 1000 of this class were built and in the late 1950s, 40 of them were still in service.

Midland Fowler 4-F Class: Introduced in 1911. By 1940 there were 772 of these engines working freight traffic.

Pacific A3: Introduced 1922. A development of Gresley's 1922 Pacific (originally classed as A-1) produced to haul the fast heavy express trains of the L.N.E.R.

Compound Class: Origin L.M.S. 1924. 6 ft 9 ins driving wheels. Worked between Leeds and Lancaster.

Royal Scot Class: Commenced service 1927. No 46113 (Cameronian) made a world's record run; taking a train non-stop from Euston to Glasgow in April, 1928, a distance of 401 miles.

Beyer-Garratt Class: Commenced service 1927. L.M.S. origin. Virtually, two 2-6-0 engines, with one boiler. There were 33 engines in the class.

Jubilee Class: Origin 1934. Designed by Sir William Stanier for express passenger service on the L.M. and Scottish Regions.

Stanier 3-MT Class: First service 1935. Number series: 40071-40209. Many based in Leeds area.

Stanier 8-F Class: Introduced 1935. Purpose: Heavy long distance freight. The majority performed their duties over the former L.M.Region.

Pacific A4: Origin 1935 for the L.N.E.R. 6 ft 8 ins driving wheels. 'Mallard' achieved a world record for steam locomotives of 126mph on 3 July 1938.

W.D. Class: Origin 1943. Austerity engine built to Ministry of Supply design as a new type of heavy traffic locomotive and saw service on all Regions except the southern.

Ivatt 2-MT Class: Origin L.M.S. 1946. Many were motor fitted for pull and push working.

Caprotti Class 5-MT: Introduced in 1948. Worked on the main lines between Leeds Bristol and Leeds St Pancras.

British Railways Standard Freight Engine 2-10-0: Built at Crewe Works. Commenced service 1954. Loco weight 86 tons, tender weight 53 tons.

THE GHOST OF BLEA MOOR TUNNEL

Dennis Howson

Senior Conductor Dennis Howson prepares to signal
the right of way on an InterCity 225 train

*A lasting memory I have of **Dennis Howson** was the time he and
I were working a Liverpool to Newcastle evening express train
between Leeds and York. At the time Dennis was the guard and
I was the ticket inspector. The train was packed with a few
hundred returning Newcastle football supporters. Soon after
departing Leeds about fifty of these people decided they would
have a bit of fun by wrecking the coaches. They were ripping
out seats, smashing windows, breaking the lights and any other
fittings that were in view and demolishing the toilets. I managed
to trap two of these villains in a first class compartment that
they had just trashed. I told them I would keep them there until
we arrived in York where the transport police would deal with
them. I was suddenly confronted by about a dozen more yobboes
who said in no uncertain terms I either let them go or I would be
beaten up. Dennis at the time was in the next coach dealing
with problems, but when he realised the predicament I was in;
he bravely fought his way through to my side to back me up. In
the event we let discretion take the place of valour and retreated
to the safety of the guard's van to await police assistance at*

York, but his actions on that evening made a lasting impression on me.

When Dennis left school, little did he think that he would spend the bulk of his working life on the railways? His first job was as a junior shop assistant, that, after a while, he realised wasn't the most exciting of jobs. Looking for something new he eventually became a coal miner at the local Peckfield Colliery. He was to stay in this job for several years until the working conditions started taking a toll on his health. Dennis left the coalmines in 1962 and spent an unsuccessful day in Leeds looking for a job. Returning to Leeds Station in a despondent mood he noticed the large railway offices in City Square and on the spur of the moment entered the building to enquire if there were any vacancies. To his astonishment he was told there was a vacancy for a porter in his own town, at Garforth Station. He was told to report to the stationmaster immediately.

Alighting from the train at Garforth, Dennis introduced himself to the stationmaster at approximately 4.0pm and after an interview lasting just a few minutes he was asked to start duty at the station on the following morning at 7.30am! He soon realised that a porter's duties at a country station were many and varied. After only two days he was acting as booking clerk, which could be very busy especially at morning and evening peak hours. Some of his other duties were dealing with parcels traffic arriving and departing from the station, attending to the signal paraffin lamps in the local area, which could be a very daunting job especially in bad weather or strong winds. He also trained to carry out local shunting duties and of course the never-ending cleaning of the station premises even to keeping the gardens neat and tidy. In 1971 he transferred to Leeds Station as a passenger guard and gained promotion to Senior Conductor with InterCity. After privatisation Dennis transferred to Virgin Trains as a Train Manager from which post he retired in 2002 having completed 40 years service.

The change in my working environment from toiling down a dark dank coal mine to employment at a pleasant country railway station could not have been more different. Right from the first day I found the job a challenge, doing the thousand and one jobs that forever were cropping up. It was certainly interesting and never boring. Taking duty at 5.30am, the first task was to light five coal fires at various locations about the station. During this time I would also be selling tickets for the first train of the day due at 5.55am. The train was known locally as the Colliers Special as it transported the Garforth coal miners to Micklefield Station for their days work at Peckfield Colliery. I would soon have a few dozen parcels to record and load onto barrows ready for the lorry driver to deliver.

I had not been working long at the station when thinking I would make life easier for myself, I thought I would take a shortcut which nearly resulted in me being killed. It was a particularly bad misty morning and I had numerous parcels on the down platform that needed to be loaded on to trains on the up platform. The correct method of carrying out this task was to load them on to a barrow and wheel them over the level barrow crossing at the platform end. I knew no passenger trains were due so I thought I could achieve the same result a lot quicker by lining them up on the edge of the down platform; dropping down onto the track and carrying them across one by one onto the up platform. I was soon engrossed in this job and positioned between the up and down mail line tracks when to my horror hurtling towards me was an express goods train. I just had time to fling myself to the ground as the train rushed past me. It could only have taken a few seconds but to me at the time I thought the end of the train would never pass. I got to my feet and was shaking so much; I had difficulty climbing back up onto the platform. I was lucky to be alive and unhurt; but it had taught me a lesson I was never to forget about taking unauthorised shortcuts on the railway!

After a while I was given the services of a 15-year-old school leaver. We were both engaged in gardening duties and had accumulated a large pile of dead wood and leaves. While I was temporarily distracted the lad decided to pour paraffin over the enormous pile and set a match to it. The result was an instantaneous surge of flame and smoke, which quickly burned down the edges dividing the station from the main road. We had several minutes of panic as we fought the fire to prevent it burning down the waiting room. I will not record in these pages what I said to the youth! Eventually I transferred to being a relief porter and could work at any one of five country stations, this was always interesting and I gained a good deal of experience about all aspects of small station working.

In 1971 I gained promotion to a passenger guard based at Leeds Station. I found I really enjoyed this type of work, in charge of local trains and parcel traffic. In 1977 I was promoted to conductor guard working long distance routes and under the Train Crew agreement of 3rd October 1988 conductor guards working for InterCity were to be known by the new title of Senior Conductor. I was to stay with InterCity until after privatisation when in 1995 I joined Virgin Trains working cross-country as Train Manager, the post from which I retired in 2002.

In the late 1970s I often worked over the Settle to Carlisle route with the old slam door stock. Enthusiasts from all over the world would come to ride over this famous railway and we guards would often have a bit of fun with them to make their day as pleasant as possible. On nearing Blea Moor tunnel (1 mile 869 yards long) I would get an unsuspecting couple to stand near the door with the drop window fully down on the pretext of seeing the mystery lights flash by the side of the train. On entering the tunnel there would be a sudden gush of water, spray into the coach, though the open window and our startled passengers would ask who had thrown the water at them. We also used to take lots of school parties on these journey's and I would often give a talk about the history of the line while making the journey north. I would also tell them about the mystery ghost of Blea Moor Tunnel who haunted the trains that passed though. I would make a pre arrangement with one of the teachers to be positioned near that particular coach light switch; and after we had entered the tunnel and while I was talking about the ghost; he would turn the lights off plunging the coach into complete darkness for a few seconds, long enough for most of them to be really scared. This was often repeated several times, much to the amusement of teachers and children.

A real life scary experience happened to me towards the end of my time working for InterCity East Coast Main Line. I was in charge of the InterCity 225 service from Leeds to London King's Cross. As we were approaching Stevenage travelling at 125 miles per hour, one of the catering staff reported a fault with one of the coach doors. I carried out an inspection and indeed the top of the door was opening and closing slightly. The Senior Conductor controls the door operation of these trains from any operating door panel along the train. Technically the doors have to be closed and an interlock engaged for the train to be able to move. I immediately rang the Control Maintenance Supervisor from my mobile phone and told him about this strange situation. He asked me to check if the door was locked. As I bent down to check the door, it suddenly flew open with the result that I nearly fell out. On arrival at King's Cross this vehicle was taken out of service for extensive tests!

On another occasion I was booked to work the *Devonian* service from Leeds to Paignton. In normal circumstances I would have gone to Neville Hill Maintenance Depot to prepare the train, but for some reason it came from the depot to the station unprepared. The train formation was loco hauled, so I proceeded from the front of the train switching on each air conditioning unit until I reached the rear, only to find that the paraffin tail lamp had not been filled. I took the lamp cleaned and filled it with paraffin and ensured a good red light was showing and attached it to the rear of the train. I then commenced walking towards the front of the train to my guard's van when the train suddenly set off on its journey to Paignton. Speaking to the Platform chargeman; I asked: 'Who is the guard of this train?' he replied: 'I don't know, I received the tip from a railman at the front.' I said: 'Well for your information I am the guard and I have not authorised this train to depart'. There was a sudden panic with desperate telephone calls until the train was stopped near Holbeck Shed. I reached the train and gave the driver the signal to depart, this time with a full train crew on board! Being a guard on a train was never a dull moment and I would have no hesitation in doing it all again if I had the chance, a really enjoyable career.

SIGNALLING IN THE STEAM AGE

On the 14th May 1990 space age technology came to York in the shape of the new state-of-the-art signalling centre. A far cry from the late Victorian days when the same area covered by the new system required dozens of manual signal boxes and scores of signalmen to work them. Too technical and complex to be called a mere signal box, its official title is: 'Integrated Electronic Control Centre' (IECC). In 2002 it took over the area previously covered by the Leeds Power Signal box and so encompassed Bradford Forster Square, Ilkley, Shipley, Skipton and on to Hellifield. On the East Coast Main Line it controls approximately 60 miles of route from just north of Doncaster to Northallerton. Among new features are Solid State Interlocking and Automatic Route Setting. All this is achieved and worked by just seven signallers and a duty shift manager.

In the early days of the railways, signalling of trains was in a very basic form. Before the advent of fixed signals, railway policemen could be positioned along a stretch of rail track to indicate to the engine driver the state of the line ahead. By the end of the 1830s the number of trains had increased and it was imperative that a more efficient form of train control be implemented. A time interval system was brought into operation. If a train had only just passed, the policeman would stop any following train by holding his arms aloft or by displaying a red flag (red light at night). After a prescribed interval of time it was assumed the train had travelled sufficiently to allow the following train to proceed. The policeman would then display to the driver a white flag (white light at night) while standing to attention.

Sound communications between those responsible for operating signals is also vital to operating a safe and efficient railway. The Navy had used semaphore signalling as a means of communication for many years before being first tried out on the railways in 1841. The need for permanent signals especially at junctions and terminal stations was essential and these early fixed signals took place in many shapes and forms. The signals were operated by a policeman, pointsman or a signal porter. By the 1850s the time interval system was becoming more and more ineffective as the volume of traffic increased throughout the country. New equipment, procedures and Rules and Regulations developed over many years. The introduction of mechanical fixed signals and the perfecting of the electric telegraph were giant steps forward in establishing the basic essentials of signalling. The next logical development was to link the mechanisms operating points and signals thereby creating interlocking. By the end of the 1860s all the elements were in place that were to remain at the core of railway signalling for the next 100 years.

Eventually semaphore signals were installed on most railways throughout the country and in the main had just two positions: DANGER when the arm was horizontal and CLEAR when the arm was at an angle of 45%. Most signals were lower quadrant but the majority of railway companies later changed to using upper quadrant. These had the advantage of being fail-safe: if a signal wire broke, the arm simply dropped to the danger position under its own weight. Separate arms were used for STOP and DISTANT signals. STOP signals had square ends and were painted RED on their faces with a white stripe, the backs being white with a black stripe. Originally the only difference between STOP and DISTANT signals was that the latter had fishtail ends. In 1925 it was decided nationally that all DISTANT signal arms should be yellow, still with the fishtail end but echoed by a black chevron near the end of the arm, the backs being white with a black chevron. An important modification was the changing of colours for signals at night. With the increasing use of street lighting it was becoming more difficult for drivers to pick out which white lights in the distance were railway signals and which to ignore. The colours were changed so that GREEN became the CLEAR signal; YELLOW was used for CAUTION and RED for DANGER.

As track layouts became more complicated and the frequency of trains increased, so the potential for accidents also increased. There was a clear requirement for a central control point for each station and junction. By bringing all controls to a central location it was also possible to link them in such a way as to prevent conflicting signals being set. Saxby & Farmer installed the first signal boxes in the early 1860s These signal boxes originally controlled only the main signals and points for an area, with the points for many local sidings still being controlled from individual levers positioned next to the points. Over a period, more and more controls were relocated to the signal boxes until all points on running lines were under the control of a signal box and only those inside yards were still controlled by the man on the ground. Signals are the vital means of informing drivers of trains about the state of the line ahead. It is, of course, important that the signals shown are correct. This is achieved by interlocking all relevant signals and points to prevent signals being shown for conflicting movements. Various forms of mechanical interlocking were used to ensure that conflicting movements could not be set up by signalmen, although each installation had to be specially built to suit its location.

The 1889 Regulation of Railways Act stipulated the use of Absolute Block working on all lines carrying passenger traffic. This meant enforcing the principle of allowing only one train at a time travelling in the same direction through a block section. No train could be allowed to follow another until the signalman at the place where the train had left the section had communicated by block instrument that the line was clear for a following train. A less restrictive form of working known as Permissive Block whereby more than one train at a time travelling in the same direction could occupy a block section was mainly used on goods and slow lines not carrying passenger traffic, and in some station platforms. The Act also required railway companies to fit all their passenger trains with continuous brakes that would operate automatically if a train became divided.

Due to the numerous different railway companies' interpreting their own set of rules, it was imperative especially after a series of accidents that a standard set of Rules and Regulations apply. Although the principles of the block system and interlocking were adopted generally, there was still a wide diversity of working practices between railway companies. Intervention by the Board of Trade was to produce complete standardisation of Rules and Regulations including terminology and bell codes, which was introduced by the end of the century. By then, mechanical interlocking, block working and the strict compliance with the Rules & Regulations made the railways of Britain as safe as any in the world.

HOLDING THE BABY

Frank Edwards M.B.E.

Frank Edwards M.B.E. in his Groundwork office

*I have known **Frank Edwards** as a friend and colleague for over 30 years. I used to call him Mr Perpetual Motion, as he never stopped working. Unlike some people who maybe need a push occasionally, Frank's chiefs would actually tell him to slow down, but he never knew the meaning of the word. Frank joined the war savaged Merchant Navy as a 16 years old in 1942 when life expectancy for these brave seamen was gauged in weeks rather than years. He had lots of frightening experiences and lost some good shipmates, but he survived the war and returned to a life ashore by joining the railways in 1948.*

His career started in the engineer's department. He progressed through various grades until in 1970 he made a breakthrough into the supervisory grade by becoming a travelling ticket inspector based at Norwich. In 1972 Frank returned to Leeds as a member of the revenue protection team, which I had joined a year before. He did have a spell as an instructor based in York, teaching guards and ticket collectors in commercial duties, but returned to Leeds to end his career as senior ticket inspector

94

in the Leeds division. He retired in 1989 after completing 41 years service. During his entire career, Frank had taken an active interest in the trade union movement and looking after the interests of his fellow workers. He was also interested in the environment and after retirement was invited to lead a project to tackle the problems of rubbish and litter on the railway bank sides and in the cuttings. Leeds City Council and British Rail funded the project jointly and Frank made such an impact and contribution that he received the top award at the Yorkshire Environmental Awards ceremony. In 1999 Frank was invited to Buckingham Palace, along with three generations of his family, to witness him receive the M.B.E. award from her Majesty Queen Elizabeth II.

In the early 1970s I joined the 7.30am Newcastle to London King's Cross train at York as a travelling ticket inspector. It was a Monday morning and this train was always very busy with businessmen and women travelling to London. My duties were to carry out a survey of people joining and alighting en route to the Capital. There was a delay in the train departing and some passengers took advantage of this by alighting from the train and purchasing drinks from the tea-bar on the adjacent platform. When the whistle sounded for the train to depart, there was a sudden rush by these passengers with drinks in their hands to rejoin the train.

As we progressed out of the platform I commenced my duties checking passengers' tickets in the first class. I had just reached a second class coach when an elderly lady approached me holding a young baby about three months old. She said the baby did not belong to her but to a young woman who she did not know, but had alighted at York, to get a cup of tea. I contacted the guard and together we searched in vain for the baby's mother. I noticed that as we were approaching Selby (we were not due to stop there) we began to slow down, so I collected the baby from the elderly lady along with a bag containing baby clothes. On arriving at Selby Station the guard brought a policewoman to the coach where I was standing.

She explained that the Transport Police at York had informed them that the mother was still on the platform when the train departed and she was now desperate to be reunited with her baby. She said that the mother was being taken by road to Selby, so I handed over the baby and accompanying bag to the police officer. On returning to the train I thanked the elderly lady for her actions in looking after the baby and then carried on with my survey. When we arrived at London King's Cross, the announcer was appealing for a soldier and gave his name, to contact the British Transport Police on platform 1 where there was a message from his wife. I noticed a soldier and said 'Are you the soldier the announcer is asking for?' He replied: 'Yes'. I took him to the police office and he was told what had happened at York and that his wife and baby would be arriving on a later train. The British Transport Police thanked me and the soldier was a very relieved man.

One of my colleagues and good friend was 'Stan the Ticket Man'; he had spent all the war years in the army on overseas service. He was a very disciplined man and always liked the job done to the letter. Having said that he was always fair when dealing with people, but he did have a big booming voice that, at times, could be intimidating to passengers. He came to me and said, 'Frank what would you have done in these circumstances?' He then told the following story. He was examining passengers' tickets on a York to Scarborough train when he came to a young lady sitting by herself and squatting under her seat was a large brown and white collie dog. When asked for her ticket she produced a valid Leeds to Scarborough ticket. Stan said: 'What about a ticket for the dog madam' she said: 'What dog?' He said, the one sitting under your seat! She said: 'Its not my dog' to which Stan said: 'It seems to know you very well'. She said 'Maybe it's just a friendly dog'!

He then asked everyone in the coach if they were the owner of the dog, but no one accepted responsibility for it. Stan was convinced the dog belonged to the lady and she was working a fast one on him. On arrival at Malton, Stan requested the duty British Transport Police officer to meet the train at Scarborough. He was even more convinced when the lady went to the toilet and the dog followed her and waited outside for her to come out. He again asked her to pay the fare for the dog. She said: 'I'm not paying for a dog that is not mine'. On arriving at Scarborough there was no police in sight and as soon as the lady opened the door, the dog shot out like a flash and she calmly followed, with the laughter of all the coach passengers ringing in Stan's ears. 'What would you have done, Frank? 'I would have put it down to experience, Stan. Remember, you can't win them all'!

Another doggy story was when I was working with a colleague called Bill on a six-coach corridor train to Doncaster. It was the day of Doncaster races and the train was very busy. Examining the tickets, we were overlapping each other and opening the compartment doors and shouting 'Tickets please'. Just outside Doncaster I heard a commotion and Bill staggered back into the corridor with blood streaming from his hand, which held his 'ticket nippers'. As soon as he had opened a door and shouted 'Tickets please', a Yorkshire terrier had jumped off the lady owner's knee and bit him. On arrival at Doncaster I took Bill to the hospital for a tetanus injection and to have the wound treated. Luckily he suffered no ill effects from the incident.

MY JOB

I'm not allowed to run the train
The whistle I can't blow
I'm not the one who designates
How far the train will go
I'm not allowed to blow the steam
Or even ring the bell
But let the damn thing jump the track
And see who catches hell!

Anon

THE WORLD OUTSIDE

1820-39: Great advances in mechanical engineering, electricity and photography. Registration of: births, deaths and marriages in England and Wales from 1837. Accession of Victoria, 1837. Penny post in England, 1839.

1840-59: Victoria marries Albert, 1840. 'Victorian Age' proper begins. Britain acquires Hong Kong after Opium War with China, 1840-2. Railways being constructed worldwide. Steam taking over from sail in ships. First Chloroform used, 1847.

1860-79: Horse drawn trams in London from 1861. Red Cross founded, 1864. Salvation Army founded, 1865. All England Lawn Tennis Championship starts at Wimbledon, 1877. First cricket Test Match between Australia and Britain, 1877.

1880-99: Electric lighting from 1880s. Henry Ford makes first car, 1893. Marconi invents radio-telegraphy, 1895. First modern Olympic games in Athens, 1896. First airship built, 1898

1900-09: First motorcycles, 1901. First British traffic laws, introduced 1903. Rolls-Royce Company founded, 1904. Boy Scout movement founded by Baden Powell, 1908. Bleriot flies the English Channel, 1909.

1910-19: Amundsen reaches South Pole, 1911; Scott, 1912. Sinking of Titanic, on maiden voyage, 1912. Woolworths founded, 1912. Start of World War I, August 1914. Population imbalances, as result of heavy war casualties, 1918.

1920-29: League of Nations founded, 1920. Lindbergh flies monoplane solo non-stop from New York to Paris, 1927. Medical advances notably in neurosurgery, tuberculosis, diabetes, tropical diseases and anaemia. Alexander Fleming discovers Penicillin, 1928.

1930-39: Radar detection set up in Britain, 1935. Edward VIII abdicates, 1936. First jet engine built by Whittle (British), 1937. Chamberlain flies to Munich; 'peace in our time', 1938. Britain declares war on Germany, 3rd September 1939.

1940-49: British army evacuated from Dunkirk, 1940. Battle of Britain in air, 1940. Pearl Harbour, 7th December 1941. Allied invasion of Europe, D-Day 6th June 1944. Germany surrenders, 8th May 1945. Major advances in antibiotics and plastic surgery.

1950-59: First suggestion of connection between smoking and lung cancer, 1953. Medical advances include antihistamines and tranquillizers. Cheaper mass-produced records begin a western world boom in 'pop music'. Pope John XXIII elected, 1959; convenes first Vatican Council since 1870.

1960-69: John F Kennedy elected President of USA, 1960. Yuri Gagarin (USSR) orbits the Earth, 1961. 'The Swinging Sixties' growth of a 'pop culture' typified by the Beatles in Britain (1962 onwards). President Kennedy assassinated, Dallas, Texas, 22nd November 1963. US astronauts land and walk on the moon, 1969.

THE TRIP OF A ICETIME

Barrie Conlon

Well turned out driver, Barrie Conlon
ready to depart for London, Kings Cross

Retired Driver **Barrie Conlon** *was to follow in the footsteps of his grandfather's brother who was an engine driver at Neville Hill Shed; his Grandfather was a guard at the same depot. Prior to joining the service, Barrie's only interest in the railway was to take the odd engine number and jot it down on a scrap of paper. From this humble beginning was sown the embryo of a career that was to span for just short of fifty years.*

It could be said that my career started with a bang as the day I joined the railway as an engine cleaner at Holbeck Shed was the 5th November 1951. Set to work in a dark smoky atmosphere with fireworks repeatedly going off, my first impression was of being in 'Dante's Inferno'. I was not allowed to work shifts until 16 years old so our hours of duty were 9am till 5pm, five days per week and an extra four hours on a Saturday morning. We worked in a gang of five cleaners and were expected to clean two locomotives per eight-hour shift for a weekly wage of £2.65. During the cleaning process we used to get absolutely filthy from the substances used to clean and remove the grease, oil, dirt and grime and many cleaners suffered from skin rashers and boils as a result of using these materials.

We never received any formal training on the steam engines but at sixteen years old we were eligible to act as fireman on the local shunt engines provided we passed an examination by the Shed Master, who at the time was Mr Geeson. He would first of all take us on the footplate of an engine where we had to show him we were competent in shovelling coal into the firebox, putting the injector on and opening and closing the dampers. On the outside we were expected to be able to name the side glands, expansion links, valve rods, state what the springs were made of and name every visible part of the locomotive. We also had to learn the Rules and Regulations in our own time.

I was to continue in this role learning all the time until I was 18 years old when I received a little brown envelope to inform me I was required to serve two years National Service. My army career was spent with the West Yorkshire Regiment in Northern Ireland and Egypt. On my return to the railway I resumed my duties at Holbeck Shed. From starting as a cleaner to becoming a fully-registered driver took nearly 28 years. Most of the time I worked with a regular driver who I got to know very well and in time when he considered me fully competent he would change places and allow me to do the driving. I always enjoyed working the specials to London St Pancras and then we would lodge overnight at Kentish Town and often work the Thames-Clyde express back to Leeds.

There were three links we worked: St Pancras, Glasgow and Birmingham. I well remember my first firing turn to Glasgow, 236 miles over the Settle Carlisle line with a Jubilee Class locomotive. I thought my driver was the coal miner's friend, as I nearly emptied the coal tender on that journey. We lodged in the Gorbals area of the City, which was not for faint hearts; but immediately I hit the bed, I was sound asleep, as the work had been really exhausting. The middle sixties saw the virtual demise of steam and so we had to learn a new form of traction with the diesel engine.

One freezing Christmas Day at this period, I reported for duty at 1.30pm to work a train to Glasgow. We were hoping to work a diesel locomotive but the shed foreman whose nickname was 'Drip Valve' because his nose was always running, said: 'You are taking a steam locomotive'. The driver and I both protested but Drip Valve using his logic said: 'If you take a diesel and it breaks down you will be stranded, a steam engine does not break down so that is what you are taking'. He gave us the Royal Scott Class 46117 'Welsh Guardsman'. The journey over the Settle to Carlisle line was bitter freezing cold and on entering Blea Moor Tunnel I was aware of a loud crunching noise above the sound of the locomotive. We soon realised what was causing this sound, when slivers of ice as thick as a man, were being broken from the roof and sides of the tunnel by our engine, came crashing onto the footplate as we both huddled together near the firebox to avoid being hit. This process was repeated at every tunnel throughout that horrendous journey. Without doubt that Drip Valve had saved our lives, as, if we had been in a diesel locomotive and these had come through the windscreen we could well have been killed.

The Deltic locomotives were introduced to the East Coast Main Line in 1961 and remained in service until early 1982. I worked on them as a second-man and often drove these monster engines between Leeds and London King's Cross. These were eventually displaced by the InterCity 125 service introduced to the ECML in 1978, which brought a new sort of comfort to driving high-powered locomotives but also demanding extreme concentration because we were travelling at a regular speed of 125mph. We also worked regular services to Newcastle, Hull and Carlisle and with the introduction of the Inter City 225 in 1989 we had yet another form of traction to learn. The Leeds and King's Cross drivers who worked these trains in the early days were responsible for ironing out the many and varied faults on the Class 91 locomotive.

I certainly enjoyed my years with the railway and had many happy hours plus a few not so pleasant experiences, like the time we were approaching Glasgow and hit two women who were trespassing on the line, one was killed outright and the other severely injured. Today, there is a vast difference between sitting in an air- conditioned electric locomotive and the exposed cab of a rolling, bucking, dusty windswept steam locomotive, but the responsibilities are still the same. I always enjoyed the company of my colleagues and the special relationship with all railwaymen but it all ended rather abruptly when I had to attend for a medical at 64. The doctor examined me and then said: 'You're finished driving trains' and within a few months I was enjoying what I considered a well-earned retirement, but could look back on a career filled with wonderful memories.

THE 'FLYING SCOTCHMAN' IN 1911

The term *Flying Scotchman* is applied to the two trains which leave Edinburgh and King's Cross, respectively, at 10.00am and perform the journey of 393 miles in 8¼ hours – an average speed of 47.64 mph. Both the up and down 'Scotchman' are duplicated during the summer months. On the up journey the 'Scotchman' stops at Berwick, Newcastle, Darlington, York and Grantham, but on the down journey the stop at Darlington is omitted. If the time standing at stations is deducted, the speed of the down train averages 50.49 mph, and that of the up train 50.82mph.

The starting time (10.00am) of these trains was fixed some 50 years ago. In February, 1859, the train leaving Edinburgh at 10.00am was due to arrive at King's Cross at 9.30pm; so that very considerable acceleration as taken place since then. Prior to November 1887, this train carried first and second class passengers only and the journey time each way performed in nine hours. After this date, third-class passengers were conveyed for the first time and this action on the part of the East Coast Companies resulted in the historic railway races of 1888 from London to Edinburgh between trains on the East and West Coast routes.

In those days there were no dining cars and the train stopped half an hour at York to allow for lunch; this during the race time was reduced to 20 minutes. On 31st August, 1888, the East Coast train performed the journey from King's Cross to Edinburgh in seven hours and 27 minutes, notwithstanding a wait of 26½ minutes at York and delays at Selby and Ferryhill. Although this is a record time for the *Flying Scotchman*, yet the actual time between London and Edinburgh was brought down to six hours 19 minutes in 1895 when the race to Aberdeen took place. The train in this instance was the 8.00pm sleeping car express from King's Cross.

It was in 1900 that dining cars were first put on to these trains (the first East Coast dining cars, however, were run in 1893 on the afternoon expresses leaving King's Cross and Edinburgh at 2.30pm) and it was in 1900 that the present time of 8 & a quarter hours was adopted. At the present time the train under normal conditions consists of eight corridor bogie vehicles weighing 280 tons with accommodation for 62 first class and 183 third-class passengers. The down train in addition conveys the travelling post office between York and Edinburgh and the up train a slip carriage from York to Doncaster.

WHAT'S IN A NAME?

The title of this article 'Flying Scotchman' *is bound to make people berate me for not checking my text. So, before someone does, I will explain my research; having exhausted the normal channels, I asked the National Railway Museum for their help. I pored over documents and finally came up with the following information. In February 1859 an East Coast express began to leave King's Cross for Edinburgh at 10.00am and at the same time another East Coast express left the old Edinburgh General Station for King's Cross. They passed each other on the wide Plain of York. The official title of the service, as far as it then had one, was* Special Scotch Express.

In the pre-railway years, a stage coach that was supposed to be faster than the general run of stage coaches was often called a 'flying coach', even though its journey lasted several days, with many unpleasant hazards. The Special Scotch Express *sooner or later became the* Flying Scotch Express, *which in turn was transformed into* Flying Scotchman *and later still when English people began to read Robert Louis Stevenson, into* Flying Scotsman. *That eventually became its official title. Still running to this day, it is by far the oldest express train in the world.*

'OFFICER, THERE ARE SHEEP IN THE FOUNTAIN'

Bill Cunliffe

Retired British Transport Police Inspector, Bill Cunliffe

I first came to know **Bill Cunliffe** *through his position as British Transport Police Inspector in the mid 1980s. As Chief Ticket Inspector at the time, I often had to liaise with the police inspectors regarding revenue protection exercises and the policing and supervision of football excursions. In the early 1990s when requiring guest speakers for the resident Senior Conductor courses held in York Hotels, it was suggested to me that we should have someone from the British Transport Police to come and talk to the students. I remembered how I had been impressed with Bill's easy manner and how he was able to communicate with people of all levels and his ability to achieve the objective with the minimum of fuss. I said to my boss; 'I know just the man' ... a phone call to Bill and thankfully he readily agreed to come and give a talk to the Senior Conductor classes that were held over a period of several months. Bill talked to the classes, straight from the shoulder and without any bull, when he had finished they had a clear view of what the police expected of them and what they could expect from the police. Bill's talks became an important part of the subsequent Senior Conductor course structure.*

106

Having no previous railway connection Bill soon set out to gain as much operating and commercial knowledge as possible to enable him to carry out his own duties to the high standard he set himself. Bill came to the British Transport Police in 1977 after serving with the Lancashire, Devon and Cornwall Police Services, based at Stretford (Old Trafford), Plymouth and East Cornwall. With the British Transport Police he served at Preston, Blackburn, Liverpool, Leeds and York. He retired in 1998 having completed a total of 30 years service and having obtained the rank of Inspector. In retirement his hobbies are caravanning, reading, history and conservation. He also works as a library assistant in Leeds and still enjoys public transport contact.

Policing can be a serious but sometimes funny experience. I have tried to focus on the funny rather than the serious and I wish to offend no one. I have decided for my part to include some unusual funny incidents and to impart some ideas as to how (1) one should never assume the obvious, (2) don't expect thanks from people, (3) rely upon good luck! The northern saying: 'Nowt as odd as folk' stood me in good stead for 30 years. In my early days I worked in Stretford, Manchester. In those days the town comprised a residential area, Manchester United Football Ground, Trafford Park Industrial Estate and the district of Old Trafford, which was being redeveloped. All the old streets were like the TV Coronation Street. A pal of mine was out on the beat one day when he saw a man climbing out of a house window in broad daylight. He recognised the man as a local thief and said: 'What are you doing Bernard?' Quickly Bernard replied: 'I heard the telephone ringing Mr Jewel and I went in to answer it!' Bernard was arrested with a minimum of fuss.

One day I was on duty in the newly built Arndale Indoor Shopping Centre, at Stretford, complete with a decorated square, fountain, fishpond and piped music. A lady approached me and said: 'Officer, there are some sheep in the square drinking water at the fountain!' Bearing in mind this was 'Urban Ville' I gave the informant an old fashioned look and said I would investigate. On arrival in the square

I was confronted with half a dozen sheep enjoying a cooling drink at the fountain. Two presents had also been deposited on the sparkling tiled floor. I was about 12 months into my service and this situation had definitely not been covered at the Police training School! Fortunately we had an officer recently transferred from Cumbria who was familiar with such goings on. He came to my aid with a Black Maria (Police Van) and between us we ushered the sheep to an exit and literally placed them in the van. We took them two miles to a farm. How on earth, six sheep, wandered that distance still confounds me!

Time passed and with it a realisation that one could always expect the unexpected. During the mid 1970s I was doing my policing in the south west of England. I was still working the streets, mainly on Panda cars. One day I received a call that a lady had locked herself out of her home. On my arrival a red faced, rather large, elderly lady met me. She went immediately on the attack asking why it had taken so long for me to arrive (10 minutes actually). The problem was she had a rather over-done roast and rice pudding in the oven, which were still cooking. I borrowed a ladder from a kindly neighbour and gained entry via a bedroom window. The distraught elderly lady was by this time bellowing instructions through the letterbox like a sergeant major! 'Open the oven-door'. 'My husband's tea is burning' and such similar instructions, all being garbled in a loud hysterical voice. I rushed to the kitchen and immediately burned my hand on the oven door (no health and safety sympathy in those days) and proceeded to remove the over-cooked food from the oven. I then let the lady into her home and far from being grateful she complained that I had spilled milk in the oven, which had burned on!

One evening I was called to a laundrette where about four or five people had been locked inside by a time lock on the door. It took two hours to trace the owner by which time we were feeding sweets and drink cartons through the letterbox. That made the local paper if my memory is correct. Moving on to my days with the British Transport Police, I recall visits to Enfield Road Sidings, Blackpool, during the night following reports of people sleeping out in the empty carriages. One night, my sergeant Ray and I visited the sidings, which had a coal yard to one side. As we wandered through the coal yard we stepped on what we assumed were empty coal sacks.... Wrong! There was a loud male and female scream and we quickly discovered two elderly vagrants were using the sacks as sleeping bags; they were covered from head to foot in coal dust. My sergeant said: 'It was like a scene from Charles Dickens'!

During the late 1970s Queen Elizabeth II was paying a visit to Preston, Lancashire, by Royal Train. I was deployed in uniform on crowd duty at the front of the now former entrance to the station. The scene was set with an excited public and flag waving school children eagerly awaiting the royal visitor who was still about ten minutes away on the train. Suddenly the crowd started cheering and waving flags. I thought: 'what's going on?' On turning round I saw the late Les Dawson (who was on his way to London) stood behind me looking absolutely shocked. I informed him of the situation whereupon he walked past the crowds waving and pulling funny faces. A true gentleman and performer. After the Queen departed I heard a child say to a teacher: 'Miss, I have seen Les Dawson and the Queen on the same day!

In the mid 1980s I moved on promotion to Liverpool where I encountered the Scouse appetite for humour. The Police Offices were located in Rail House where the Divisional Manager's staff were also based. Within Rail House was a mailroom and the duties of the staff employed there at night was to sort the mail and ensure the security of the building. One such member of staff was known on occasions to snatch forty winks in the small hours prior to his security sweep at dawn. A police officer that shall remain anonymous took it upon himself to visit the mailroom during such a snooze, equipped with black boot polish, whereupon he gave the individual a makeover. When the individual visited the police offices some two hours later it took considerable effort not to laugh. He was completely unaware of his new-found self. I heard that he was none too pleased when he finally looked in a mirror, but it probably cured him of sneaking forty winks.

I was talking to a colleague recently and he recalled a visit of the late Princess of Wales to Saltaire by Royal Train. Saltaire Station is very small and relatively easy to contain. My colleague and I along with many others were maintaining a security cordon when the Royal Train arrived. Suddenly, a stray dog appeared from between legs and wondered along the platform train side, stopped and did a whoopsie near to where the Princess was alighting. The Princess, being a true professional, merely looked the other way.

During one of my spells at York I received a report that an armed man was on a London to York bound train. Armed officers arrived and put a ring of steel round the station. On arrival of the train a little old lady alighted and came to me and said: 'What's all the fuss about?' And she calmly stated that the man had alighted at Doncaster and he had never had a gun! End of operation!

One day I was stood at the front of Leeds Station. The traffic was very heavy with buses and taxis all awaiting the arrival of trains. I was in uniform along with a very dry humoured Yorkshire sergeant nearing the end of his career. A chap walked up and said: 'Could you tell me the quickest way to Leeds Infirmary? Without flinching and in broad Yorkshire replied: 'Certainly Sir. Step in front of that bus!' Even the chap laughed at the effortless reply. Suffice to say he was given the correct directions.

THE BRITISH TRANSPORT POLICE

The construction of a railway was a great engineering project and involved the employment of thousands of men, who had to live near the construction sites and move on as the railway progressed. The maintenance of law and order on the line of the railway under construction in areas where there were no police at all had to be undertaken. In consequence the railway companies obtained special Parliamentary Powers to authorise Justices to appoint Railway Constables.

When passengers and merchandise began to move along the railways the greatest social changes experienced in Britain began to take place. The country had emerged not long before from the Napoleonic Wars and conditions were very unsettled. Not only the merchandise but also the railway installations were often interfered with and serious losses occurred.

The first mention of a Railway Police Establishment is in connection with the Liverpool and Manchester Railway in 1830: 'The Police establishment have station houses at intervals of a mile along the road. These stations form also the depots for passengers and goods from or to any of the intervening places. The duties assigned to these men are to guard the road to prevent or give notice of any obstructions and to render assistance in the case of any accident and to do this effectively to keep up a continual line of communication'.

According to a Rule Book of 1838 the policemen's duties consisted of:

the preservation of order in all the stations and on the line of railway...; to give and receive signals; to keep the line free from casual or wilful obstructions; to assist in the cases of accidents; to caution strangers of danger on the railway; to remove intruders of all descriptions; to superintend and manage the course and switches; to give notice of arrivals or departures; to direct persons into entrances to the stations or sheds; to watch movements on embankments or cuttings; to inspect the rails and

111

solidity of the timber; to guard and watch the Company's premises; and to convey the earliest information on every subject to their appointed station or superior officer.

The present-day British Transport Police are the successors to these police forces. It is the national police force for the railways, providing a policing service to rail operators, their staff and passengers throughout England, Wales and Scotland. The Force is also responsible for policing the London Underground system, the Docklands Light Railway, the Midland Metro Tram System and the Croydon Tramlink. Between them, these rail businesses move some five million people every day. The railway environment presents its own particular policing needs and the British Transport Police, which at present numbers in excess of 2,100 police officers and over 560 civilian support staff, exists to provide a specialist policing service to meet those needs.

Policing the railways is an integral part of policing the community and the Force forms part of the national policing structure which safeguards the citizen. The majority of the Force's activity, like that of any other police force, is law and order and protecting staff and public. During the early years, Constables had specific responsibility for the surrounding area as each Constable was sworn in as a County Constable as well as a railway company police officer. Nowadays, the Force is constantly giving help to, and receiving help from, local forces to provide the best possible service to its customers. Every duly appointed member of a Police Force in Britain is a Constable whatever his rank in the Force. He holds the office of Constable. He is an Officer of the Law. He has certain special powers and he also has certain responsibilities. A Constable of the British Transport Police serves the Sovereign in the office of constable and is in addition in a special position by virtue of his appointment as a servant of the British railways. Every member of the Force must either be in uniform or provided with an authority to act before he attempts to carry out the duties of his office.

In the late 19th century, the continually spreading rail network gave criminals new opportunities to move around the country. Crime and criminals do not hesitate to cross county boundaries and crime can be committed on the move with rapid means of escape. The network nature of the railway system also means that incidents affecting its operation in one location can reverberate down the system, creating knock on effects for thousands of people many miles away. This is why the railway has special policing needs and why a national police force for the railways is a cost effective solution.

Nowadays, British Transport Police makes full use of modern technology to track, prevent and detect crime across the nation. A major reorganisation of the Force's structure was carefully planned and implemented in April 1992. Throughout its history, the force has evolved to meet the increasing demands of the industry it polices. The present organisation is designed to deliver the best possible value for money to the rail industry and its users.

*It's all DMU's at the west end of Leeds City South on
9th May, 1962, except for 4MT tank 42189, which is coming off
the Empty Coaching Stock it brought from Neville Hill.*

*Easter Monday, 23rd April, 1962 and Neville Hill B1 61030
'Nyala' has an additional 12.55pm Selby out of Leeds City South.*

On the 4th September, 1960, the Railway Correspondence and Travel Society ran a special train with preserved Midland Compound engine 1000. It is seen here passing over the recently rebuilt bridge over the canal and through Leeds City Junction, on the downfast line.

One of the many empty mineral wagon trains worked up the Midland main line comes through Whitehall Junction on 15th August 1961, headed by '8F' 48721.

115

A4 60032 'Gannet'heads the 5.17pm Leeds Central - Doncaster up the grade at Copley Hill on 1st Septmber 1961. She is just doing enough to overtake Black 5 45204 hauling a Neville Hill - Copley Hill freight on the 'Wessie'.

46493 shunting some vans at Leeds City North, South Sidings. Watching progress is Carriage Shunter Joe 'Wop' in his shiny jacket on the 19th April, 1962.

The Geldard signalman keeps his eye on A1 60157 'Great Eastern' pushing its train up the incline to 'B' box. 4MT tank 42324 was on the other end, ready to give a push, after reversal on 5th June, 1962.

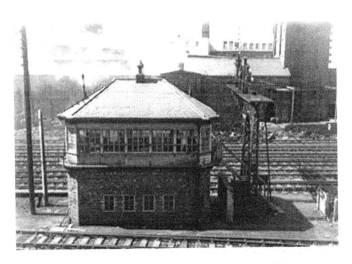

Marsh Lane signal box on 8th June, 1964.

117

Engine Shed Junction, as seen from Nineveh Road bridge on 22nd June, 1964. 9F 92103 has the road on the up main line.

B1 61062 has come off shed at Neville Hill East to assist 8F 48758 to work the Newcastle - Redbank Stock over to Manchester on 20th July, 1964.

THE PORK PIE CLERKS

Graham Briggs

Trains Inspectors Graham Briggs (left) and Dave Wilson
check the environmental Panel on an InterCity 225 train

*I first met **Graham Briggs** on the 6ᵗʰ January 1988 at the
prestigious Viking Hotel, York. The occasion was the initial
gathering of 21 men who would, after training, form the new
grade of Trains Inspectors for the Eastern Region. The team
came from as far away as King's Cross, Newcastle and all points
in-between. We were to embark on an intensive three and a half
weeks training course, no day of which was ever less than twelve
hours! During this period Graham and I became good friends
both in a working environment and during social gatherings.
We found we had the same enthusiasm for the job and the same
standards and outlook in our private lives. Graham was not a
long-time serving railwayman; in fact he only joined the railway
in 1974 and completed just 22 years before his retirement in
1996. In railway parlance he had hardly got his number dry,
but he was soon to make an impression and climb the promotional
ladder.*

119

Born in Gravesend, North Kent, just across from the Tilbury Docks, it was no wonder Graham came from a sea-faring family. His father served on a merchant ship that was torpedoed during World War II. Leaving school at 15 years he served a five-year apprenticeship to become an electrical engineer. He then joined the Merchant Navy serving on the 30,000-ton cruise liner SS Iberia as an electrical officer. On one such cruise in the Mediterranean Ocean he met a young lady passenger called Aileen. From that initial meeting blossomed a romance with the result they have now been happily married for 40 years and have two sons, one of whom is carrying on the railway tradition as a Driver Standards Manager based at Brighton. After five years service Graham came ashore to work for the Yorkshire Electricity Board for the next ten years.

He always had a strong interest in the railways and one day he saw a newspaper advertisement for freight guards. He filled in his application, was accepted and commenced his railway career at Immingham Freight Depot. After training he was to serve seven years as a freight guard. He then transferred to Cleethorpes working passenger trains and eventually became the station supervisor. In January 1988 he was promoted to the new grade of trains inspector based at Hull. A year later he transferred to Leeds as senior trains inspector. His final move in 1994 was to the York based headquarters of InterCity as 'on train safety and technical support manager' from which position he took early retirement in 1996 in order to concentrate on his passion for golf.

I commenced my railway career on the 22nd July 1974 as a trainee freight guard at Immingham Freight depot (40B). I was sent on a six weeks Rules and Regulations course at the Guards School at Doncaster. The instructor was called Vic Lee and for someone like me, who was joining the railway 'off the street' so to speak, you could not have wished for a better introduction to the intricacies of railway workings. Vic had the natural ability to pass on his years of railway experience in a most interesting and informative manner. Little did I know a few years later I would be working alongside Vic, but more about that later.

Having passed in the Rules and Regulations examination it was back to Immingham to commence 'road learning'. This not only included all the main line working but the large complexes at Immingham and Grimsby. We were also required to learn the Grimsby Light Railway, which linked the Immingham and Grimsby docks and large freight yards. Road learning was undertaken under the guidance of old hand guards who would impart their years of knowledge and experience on to you and I can say was greatly appreciated. I still have my road-learning book, which was self-compiled showing all the signals, points, gradients and landmarks of the particular route. It was most important to know the gradients because we were still working unfitted (loose-coupled) trains, that is trains not fitted with automatic brakes on the wagons; only the locomotive and guard's van had brakes; the wagons only had a crude parking brake, which had to be manually operated.

Before commencing any journey the guard had to prepare the train and calculate the weight, length and maximum speed allowed. This information was entered onto a 'driver's slip' and was handed to the driver, when we would then discuss how we would work the train and apply the brakes. This was important to having an efficient smooth running journey. While road learning I was also gaining knowledge in train operation and how to know where we were in dark or foggy conditions. There was no pressure to 'sign' a road, only when you were absolutely confident, would you then, 'sign' for it on your personal route card.

My first solo trip was working a train of iron-ore from Immingham Docks to Scunthorpe Steel Works. The train consisted of two Class 27 locomotives working in multiple and twenty-one 100-ton rotary tippler wagons giving a tonnage of 2310 tons. These at the time were the heaviest trains in the United Kingdom and timed to run at 60mph. The train was a class 6, fully fitted; that is with the automatic air brake fitted to every wagon and controlled by the driver, which meant that the guard rode on the locomotive. The journey passed without incident but I can still remember how uneasy I was and kept thinking of all the Rules and Regulations and what action I would have to carry out if any incident occurred. By this time, most trains were fully fitted and class 7 and 8 (loose coupled) trains, where the guard rode in a brake van at the rear of the train were being phased out.

At weekends we could be called upon to work 'ballast trains'. These were used by the civil engineers to carry out track repairs and maintenance, designated class 9 and timed to run at 25mph. Looking back to travelling round the country in a brake van, it is hard to believe that up until the late 1970s we still had one tail and two side lights which were illuminated by paraffin. The heating was by a coal burning stove. We had moved on to an electric Bardic hand lamp, but to be in a 'Queen Mary' brake van with a coal fire and the stove pipe glowing cherry red and your brew can simmering on the stove still gives me a warm feeling to this day.

One of the rostered turns at Immingham was a twice weekly run to New Holland Pier with coal for the Humber ferries to Hull. There were three boats: Lincoln Castle, Tattershall Castle and Wingfield Castle; all were built in the early 1940s. These boats carried both vehicles and foot passengers. On this particular journey my train consisted of a class 47 locomotive and 16-ton wagons with a brake-van at the rear. Due to the layout at New Holland Pier the train required two guards and because this was my first trip I was the assistant guard. Also at New Holland was a siding called Oxmarsh, from which a coal merchant operated and his coal was conveyed along with the ferry coal.

The pier at New Holland was about a quarter of a mile into the River Humber and consisted of three roads. The left side road was for the Barton on Humber DMU shuttle service. The right side road was for the Grimsby / Cleethorpes services and the middle road was the coal road. There were no stop blocks on the coal road and as the coal wagons were propelled along this route I was always fearful of them ending up in the river. The experienced guard

explained to me how we would carry out the shunting ma
but also informed me that by far the biggest hazard was ave
Viking Helmets and the Walnut Whips. When I enquired w.
were he replied: 'You will soon find out'. The ferry crew who   ¬id
unload the coal from the wagons met us on arrival at the pier. Stepping
down from the train onto the pier I soon discovered the meaning of
Viking Helmets and Walnut Whips as I stepped into a pile of human
excreta. This was because passengers were continually using the
toilets while the trains on each side of the coal line were stood.

The guard told me that the coal merchant's wagons were in the
wrong part of the train but to save a lot of shunting he would change
the wagon labels of the ferry coal with the merchants coal wagons
thus making things very easy for us. He said that's how you save
yourself a lot of work. On the return journey I had to remove my
shoes and tie them up outside the brake van; I have never fancied a
Walnut Whip since. Two days later I was asked by the inspector if I
had been on the New Holland job on the Tuesday as there had been
a complaint from the coal merchant that he had received inferior
coal which was only good for ferry services. When I entered the
mess-room the guard who had altered the labels was writing out a
'please explain' and muttering that he did not know about different
grades of coal.

(Footnote: The ferry service ceased to operate in July 1981 with the
opening of the Humber Bridge. All three ferries have been
preserved.)

By the late 1970s I had progressed to the 'top link' at Immingham.
During the summer months one of our duties was to provide cover
for the passenger guards depot at Cleethorpes. Being a seaside resort
there was always lots of seasonal trains to be worked. So, after
learning coaching stock and diesel multiple units, it was my introduction
to revenue protection by making sure every passenger had a valid
ticket. To ensure I was up to this task I was sent on a ticket course
at Doncaster, which I found was extremely interesting. I found

working with passengers to be, on the whole, most enjoyable and I was to spend many happy hours at Cleethorpes.

Eventually a vacancy occurred for a passenger guard at Cleethorpes, so I decided to apply. At that time promotion to a passenger guard was based on a person's seniority date. (This was all to change with the introduction of the Train Crew Agreement on 3rd October 1988 when suitability was brought into the selection to fill a vacancy.) On my third application I was informed that I had obtained a position as passenger guard and my transfer date would be 1st June 1981. Cleethorpes was only a small train crew depot with 26 guards, compared with 120 guards at Immingham. The drivers were based at Grimsby Docks Station. There were no night duty turns, the first booking on time was 4.30am and the last booking off time was 12.15am.

I settled down to the life of a passenger guard. It was a most enjoyable job, meeting different passengers every day and there was always the challenge of dealing with a few people who seemed to think they could travel on the trains without paying the fare. By this time the direct service from Cleethorpes to London King's Cross had been reduced to one a day – departing at 6.20am, the return service from King's Cross left at 6.18pm. Class 47 diesel locomotives and mark II coaching stock worked them. In October 1982 InterCity East Coast introduced the High Speed Train (HST) to this service and it cut the journey time by 45 minutes, so it was a return to the Doncaster Training School and Neville Hill Maintenance Depot for an HST Training course.

I had the dubious honour of working the first HST into Cleethorpes, having relieved a Peterborough guard at Newark Northgate; this service lasted until May 1993 when the through service to King's Cross was withdrawn. Little did I know when I brought the first HST service into Cleethorpes I would also be on the last HST into that station but by this time I was Senior Trains Inspector at Leeds. Towards the end of 1985 I was still enjoying my time as a passenger guard but a vacancy had arose for a station supervisor at Cleethorpes. After much thought I decided to apply as I wished to broaden my railway knowledge. Interviews were held in January 1986 consisting of a panel of three, with each interview lasting one hour. Within days I was informed I had been successful in my interview and would start training in two weeks time. It was with mixed feelings that on a Sunday evening I worked my last train into Cleethorpes, all the time thinking of all the journeys and good times I had enjoyed while being a guard, not to mention my apprehension as to what the future would hold for me in my new position in the salaried grade.

The next morning I commenced my training as a station supervisor, which involved a three-shift system over seven days. It was my first introduction to man management skills because, apart from the 26 guards, there were 16 carriage cleaners, shunters and rail men to manage. There was invariably the problem of dealing with late-running trains and failure of train units and locomotives. The night shift was always busy with all trains requiring cleaning and fuelling. Although I missed travelling about on trains I did enjoy the new job and the challenge it brought each day. I thought at the time that I would probably see out my career in this post. However, in late 1987 it was decided by the Eastern Region to set up a new department called the Trains Inspectorate. I would equate this to the drivers' Traction Inspectors. These inspectors would be based at various locations along the Eastern Region and for the first time give the guards their own management team. One of these posts was located at York but based at Hull and would also cover the guard's depots at Bridlington and Scarborough; should I apply?

Yes I did and after numerous tests, selection procedures and interviews I was eventually advised I had been appointed to the Hull post. So at the end of 1987 it was again with mixed feelings that I worked my last shift at Cleethorpes. In January 1988 21 men who would form the new team of trains inspectors met in an hotel in York to begin what was to become a very intensive training course lasting 12 hours a day over several weeks. One of the instructors was Vic

Lee who had set me off on my railway career and again he helped make the course very enjoyable. This was an exciting time, being part of a new concept and so at the end of the course, we then had to pass an examination in Rules and Regulations at a higher level so that we could undertake the guards' biennial examination. We were now embarking on a new era of train working and our small team had a direct involvement in the day-to-day running of trains.

My office was in Paragon House, above Hull Station, which I shared with Ray Preston the Traction Inspector. So we started the job of setting new standards for guards in their operating and revenue protection roles and, pleasing to say, after some initial opposition they soon realised we were there to help them in their duties and we soon gained their confidence. I was at Hull until July 1989 when a new post was created for a Senior Trains Inspector working for InterCity East Coast based at Leeds. I applied for this post and after an interview I was appointed to this position.

My move to Leeds was in July 1989, and I was to work with Peter Kirton, another Senior Trains Inspector. This was the start of a working and personal friendship, which still lasts to this day. It soon became obvious that both Peter and I shared the same values and ideas on how we raised the standards at Leeds. There was a heavy workload to get through. The guards at Leeds were required to have extensive road knowledge. The routes were: Leeds - King's Cross, Leeds – Newcastle, Leeds – Carlisle, and during the summer months an HST service from York to Scarborough on Saturdays. We were required to travel with every guard at least twice a year to check on their ability to carry out all of their duties in a competent manner. We also had to take each guard on a full day Rules and Regulations examination every two years. With the introduction of the new InterCity 225 train in October 1989 the guards all had to be trained and passed as qualified to work this service.

In October 1988 the guards had been renamed, those working for Regional Railways were known as 'conductors' and those working for InterCity were known as 'senior conductors' but in the rule book they were still referred to as 'guards'. In 1991 Peter Kirton was promoted and moved to York Headquarters as the Route Chief Trains Inspector. I then took over the running of Leeds and Doncaster senior conductor depots with two trains inspectors to assist me. It was at this time I was getting involved with Peter in training senior conductors who were joining the various InterCity routes. Their course consisted of a three-week residential programme based in a Swallow Hotel. We travelled the length and breadth of the country to carry out these duties.

On one particular course at the Swallow Hotel, Grantham, after Peter had signed in and gone to his room, I told the receptionist in a serious voice that he was on release from Rampton Mental Hospital and on no account were the female staff to speak or go near him. She said, I thought he looked a bit strange. We were there for three days and when we were checking out Peter said to the receptionist: 'I don't know what I have done to your staff but none of them have come near me or attempted to make conversation all the time I have been here'. The receptionist said: 'I am sorry about that sir' and then gave me a knowing wink. It wasn't until we were on the train going home that I let Peter in on the secret.

On another occasion we were staying at the Great Northern Hotel at King's Cross. I approached Peter who was talking to a West Indian lady chambermaid. Peter introduced me as a doctor and said I had a lovely bedside manner and naturally I went along with the pretence. The next day I met the same chambermaid who was rather buxom and she said; 'Oh doctor, I keep getting an irritation in my bosom; I wander if you would mind examining me please. It is not often I am lost for words so, like all good reporters, I made my excuses and beat a hasty retreat.

During 1992 Peter was ill and I was asked to cover his duties, this gave me a 'patch' of 524 miles (London King's Cross – Aberdeen) with senior conductor depots at King's Cross, Doncaster, Leeds,

Newcastle, Edinburgh, Glasgow and Aberdeen. This role was to liaise with the trains inspectors at all these depots to make sure that the high standards of InterCity East Coast were maintained. Another duty was to accompany all V.I.Ps travelling on InterCity services. On the 25th September 1992 I carried out one of these duties. It was to escort the National Military Representatives from the Supreme Headquarters Allied Powers Europe on their annual visit to the United Kingdom. We departed King's Cross at 8.00am on the Scottish Pullman with a special stop order for Northallerton Station so the party could visit RAF Leeming for the day. All of Coach K was reserved for the party along with attendant security. After breakfast Brigadier General George-Heinrich Roth from Germany called on me to accept a plaque in appreciation of the service provided by InterCity. I responded, thanking them and explained that I was only part of a team that it took to produce the train service. The plaque is still on display in my lounge. In the late afternoon I escorted the party from Northallerton back to King's Cross. I eventually arrived home after a long, long day but one I shall always remember.

At the start of 1994 it was decided to merge the operating and catering functions on train. The trains inspectors' would be called trains service managers and they would supervise the senior conductors and the catering crews. I was appointed to undertake the operating type training, which the new organisation would require and I would be based at York HQ. It was a similar role to which Peter Kirton had carried out but he had now taken early retirement. The new organisation would consist of a 50/50 split between operating and catering and the latter group would require intensive Rules and Regulations courses. I could see that this role would be very demanding to convert, in the nicest sense, 'pork pie clerks' into operators. I had a meeting with Alex Gibb the Route Trains Manager who was very keen about the project. It took me about me ten seconds to say I would undertake the project. I came away from the meeting as the On Train Safety and Technical Support Manager for InterCity East Coast, so it was back to the 524 mile patch again.

I put together the Rules and Regulations courses and carried them out in Doncaster and Edinburgh and, to their credit, the 'pork pie clerks' were very keen to learn. I still smile when I think back at the first question I used to ask them: 'What do you think the senior conductors' role and responsibilities are?' I always got the same response: 'Press the buzzer to start the train and check a few tickets'! A few weeks later when they were deemed ready to sit an examination, they had changed their views somewhat. My next project was to train senior conductors in the new central locking system that had been installed on slam-door stock operated by InterCity (on mostly InterCity 125s). I had a demonstration coach based at Doncaster for this purpose. At this time I was also on-call one week in three so the time seemed to fly by.

Following problems at King's Cross, I was invited to take over the running of the senior conductor depot. I therefore became a long distance commuter. I would leave home at 6.30am, drive over the Humber Bridge to Brough Station where I would catch the 7.15am Hull – King's Cross service. Often I would help the catering crew and even mastered poring out coffee while travelling at 125 mph. Returning home I would travel on the 5.20pm King's Cross – Hull service, arriving at Brough at 7.35pm, drive back over the bridge and arrive at my home at 8.10pm, a very long day. Little did I know when I took on this task I would continue in this role until I took early retirement on the 12th October 1996, just before my 58th birthday. It was a challenge at King's Cross but they were good people to work with and had a professional approach to the job, which soon showed in the improvement of the depot.

With the approach of privatisation I thought the time right for me to take early retirement and so when the opportunity arose I decided with a certain amount of reluctance to accept it. I would like to take the opportunity to thank my wife Aileen for putting up with all the unsocial hours I had to work, never knowing when I would be coming home and all the long periods spent away, but as the Frank Sinatra song goes: It's nice to go travelling, but it's much, much nicer to come home.

COP FOR COVA

Passenger: 'How long will the next train be?' Railman: about 250 feet.

Advice to young, novice clerk by senior booking clerk: If a passenger leaves his change behind, you should immediately attract his attention by rapping smartly on the window with the office sponge.

A lady was travelling to Dent Station on the Settle to Carlisle line. On arrival at Dent, she alighted and seeing nothing but countryside around her, asked the guard 'Where is the village of Dent? The guard replied 'It is about three miles away, down the hill'. The lady then asked 'Wouldn't it have been better to build the station nearer to the village?' To which the guard replied, 'Yes madam, but we thought it better to build it nearer the railway'.

One of the most dangerous times for a train is when braking just as a shower of rain starts. The light sprinkling of water on the rail mixes with the oil and grease from passing trains and produces a lethal surface similar to that of an ice rink. As soon as the driver, touches the brakes; the wheels lock and slide along the rails. The speedometer in the cab suddenly drops from 50mph to 0mph and you know there is nothing you can do. If you apply the emergency brake, more wheels lock further along the train and the slide just damages more wheels. If you release the brake, you won't stop where you are supposed to. If you let things stay as they are, you won't stop where you are supposed to anyway. You might just as well 'drop the lot' and let the train stop where it will. At least everyone will hear all the air escaping from the brake pipe and see that at least you tried. The fact that the whole train set of wheels will have developed flats is not your concern at the moment!

Driving cabs are the coldest places on the railway. They are stuck at the front of the train roaring through the winter weather with nothing more than a piece of metal and glass protecting the person driving the thing. Heaters are usually designed to prevent the equipment from freezing and would not meet animal protection requirements, let alone human comfort needs. However, all is not lost. The imaginative driver can improve his 'office' comforts with various uses of newspapers.

Newspapers are essential for stuffing in all the cracks, splits and openings, which always appear in a cab, no matter how well designed or maintained the cab is, and most are not. Newspapers are also good for lining the inside of your boots – they make a very good insulator. When rolled into a ball and rubbed into the dust on the cab floor, they are useful for cleaning the oil and grease off the windows, which always appear when it starts to rain. Remember, train cleaners, still clean windows with an oil soaked rag. Newspaper is essential if you are getting under a train for any reason, like releasing brakes, draining reservoirs, pulling fuses, oiling, isolating anything or tying anything down. The underneath of a train is always filthy and you don't want to get grease and dirt on your hands and then leave it all over the controls when you get back in the cab. Finally, in an extreme emergency, lay a few pages on the floor, sprinkle liberally with sand and you have a quick, environmentally friendly, disposable toilet! Finally, an essential article of clothing for the locomotive driver in the winter is a black plastic bag. When required, place both legs inside the bag and tie loosely with string. It makes an excellent leg warmer, as was demonstrated by Leeds Driver John Poskitt, on a London journey and filmed by BBC1 Television, 1st May 1991.

A DOG CALLED LUCKY

Joe Lomax

Senior Conductor Joe Lomax keeping the passengers informed
14th September 1995

*Senior Conductor **Joe Lomax** was born in a small village just outside Whitby, but most of his school years were spent at Darlington. Leaving school at 15 years, Joe was undecided on what his future was, until he saw a group of men working at the North Road Locomotive Works. After a brief conversation with the foreman his future was sealed when he was taken on as a tea boy at the Faverdale Maintenance Works. After approximately one year he transferred to Darlington Station to take on another job, which has long passed into history, as a, call out knocker-upper. Part of his equipment for this job was a long pole with a brass hook; to tap on the upstairs window of the person required to take duty. His next job was as a relief porter, being sent anywhere in the area to cover vacancies and sickness. The jobs were many and varied, sometimes assisting a freight guard shunting his train, filling and trimming the brake van paraffin lamps, sorting parcel traffic for local distribution, going out to farms in the Catterick and Leyburn area to deliver empty milk churns and returning with full ones.*

At 18 years Joe received his call-up for National Service, serving with the Royal Engineers. He enjoyed the life so much that he stayed on for six years, serving in Germany, the Middle East and Far East. He returned to the railways in 1968 employed as a porter at Leeds Station and then moving on to be a freight guard and finally a senior conductor with InterCity.

When working as a Senior Conductor for InterCity I always assumed I could deal with all the different types of passengers we met up with in our journeys between Leeds and London King's Cross. We often had over 400 passengers on these trains and there was usually one or two who were looking for an argument, but I nearly always managed to talk them round and leave them happy. However, on one journey to King's Cross I really met my match in the form of an 80-year-old lady. She had joined the train at Leeds and was travelling to Grimsby. When asked for her ticket she produced a senior citizen railcard and said she wished to purchase a cheap ticket. I told her she should have purchased a cheap ticket before boarding the train, as I was not allowed to sell cheap tickets on the train. The old lady did not take this news very well at all, and she proceeded to tell me, and the rest of the coach; that I was upsetting and victimising an old lady. She would not let up her verbal abuse of me, and followed me to the end of the coach. We were now arriving in Doncaster but I announced over the public address to the whole train that we were arriving in Grimsby! The old lady had managed to make me upset every passenger on the train. It was then I decided to break the rules and sell her the cheap ticket!

On another occasion I was working with a colleague who came to a family of ten Chinese, adults and children. They were seated in the bargain first coach that at the time carried a supplement of £10 per person, irrespective of being child or adult. My colleague said to the head of the family; 'If you want to stay here the excess is £10 per person so the total is £100' to which the Chinese man replied: 'Why should I pay you that amount?' The senior conductor replied 'Why should I pay 80 pence, every time I buy fried rice?

The train pulled up at the branch line unmanned station. The only person to board the train was a man in his early thirties, carrying a travel bag. I was just going to ask for his ticket but he disappeared into the toilet. We called at a couple more stations where people joined the train and I sold them tickets or inspected the ones they already had. I suspected that the man still in the toilet was trying to travel without paying his fare so, after 15 minutes, I knocked on the door and shouted: 'Ticket please sir'. There was no reply, so after a couple more minutes I knocked again: 'Ticket please sir'. The door slowly opened to reveal a woman heavily made up with lipstick and mascara, dressed in a mini skirt with fishnet stockings and carrying the same travel bag. I checked that the toilet was empty and then said to the person: 'Ticket please madam!

One April Fools day the senior conductor went on to the public address and said: 'Ladies and Gentlemen I have a special announcement to make, a lady travelling in coach B has lost her dog and it is believed to be somewhere in the train. I have a description; it is brown and white, only has one eye, just half of his left ear, his right rear leg is heavily bandaged and he answers to the name of Lucky'!

Working between Leeds and London King's Cross every day was always interesting and some regular passengers we got to know very well. There were ups and downs while working these services but on the whole the job was really enjoyable. The end came for me when due to ill health I had to take early retirement, but I will always have happy memories of my time with the railways and the special friendships with hundreds of colleagues.

RAILWAY MILEPOSTS

1812: Matthew Murray's steam locomotive begins service on the Middleton Railway Leeds, and is an immediate commercial success.

1814: George Stephenson builds his first locomotive 'Blucher'.

1825: Stockton and Darlington Railway opened.

1829: Stephenson's Rocket wins the Rainhill trials.

1841: The Manchester and Leeds Railway opens, first across the Pennines.

1856: John Saxby patents interlocking of points and signals.

1878: River Tay Bridge opens: Collapsed during a gale the following year.

1889: The Regulation of Railways Act receives Royal Assent.

1890: Opening of The Firth of Forth Bridge. World's biggest cantilever bridge.

1915: A human rather than a signalling failure, it caused a double collision at Quintinshill, north of Carlisle. With 224 deaths it was the worst railway disaster in Britain.

1923: Formed under the Railways Act of 19th August 1921, 123 British railway companies are amalgamated to form four groups from 1st January 1923: Southern, London Midland and Scottish, Great Western, London and North Eastern.

1928: The London and North Eastern Railway commence operating the longest non-stop run in the world from London to Edinburgh.

1938: Mallard achieves the world speed record for a steam engine between Grantham and Peterborough.

1948: The rail network of Britain becomes nationalised on 1st January 1948.

1952: Britain's worst peacetime rail disaster at Harrow and Wealdstone. A signal was passed at danger during fog and 112 were killed.

1954: Diesel multiple units first operated nationwide.

1955: First of the 'Deltics' produced.

1968: Last of steam traction from British Rail lines.

1983: British Rail sells off its last hotel, the Queen's in Leeds.

1987: The High Speed Train (HST) achieves a world speed record for a diesel: 148mph.

1994: The Queen and President Mitterand open the Channel Tunnel on 6th May.

TWO FOR THE PRICE OF ONE!

Ralph Waggett

A Ticket to Ride - issued by booking clerk, Ralph Waggett

My workday memories of **Ralph Waggett** *are of a jovial man who always went out of his way to help anyone. He was one of the many unsung heroes of British Rail, who went about his job without fuss or favour. Ralph did not originate from a railway family but once he joined the ranks, he was to give 42 years dedicated service to the Company. His first job as a 16-year-old Grammar School leaver was as an office boy. Seeking a little more excitement he joined the Royal Navy to see the world, and served as an ordinary seaman aboard the light cruiser HMS Cleopatra. On demob he thought he would try to become a policeman but failed because he was half an inch too short. He was advised to try for the railway police and at the same time applied for a position as a railway clerk, thinking that whichever was offered to him a job first he would take. Well, the clerical grade won. His career commenced as a junior clerk at Drighlington Station (now a traffic roundabout) from where he was to discover the oddities not only of the workplace but also of his boss who worked there. His next move was to Thornton Station, now long gone, before moving as a relief clerk to Leeds.*

137

His next spell was at Bradford Forster Square where he gained experience working at numerous stations around the area. Returning to Leeds he worked in the Divisional Headquarters as a claims clerk before gaining further promotion as Chief Clerk at Halifax Station. His final move and from where he retired in 1990 was the Area Manager's Office at Leeds.

My first job was at Drighlington Station, which in its day was quite busy. It was situated on the old Great Northern line between Bradford and Wakefield. The Station Master was an old-fashioned long-serving man who pretended to be deaf! The office telephone was a G.P.O. pay phone and all outward calls had to be paid for, so the SM would call a major inquiry if such a call were made without his permission. If a call came for him when he was out on the platform, no amount of calling would attract his attention. I was so frustrated one day, calling him in vain, I turned to the porter and said in a soft voice. 'He is a deaf, daft, silly old sod'. He must have heard that all right, because he immediately turned to me and gave me a good telling off.

The smaller stations were immaculate, the brass work in the office shone. I particularly recall Ingrow West on the Worth Valley Line. The place was an absolute picture. I enjoyed my time at Thornton Station on the Bradford to Keighley G.N. line. That was a very busy place for goods traffic and parcels. We would ask the engine drivers for some coal for the office stove and they would toss half a ton of it on to the platform. The Station Master was another of the old school insisting that the station name was called out for every train that stopped there. He died recently aged 97 years.

People still reminisce fondly about steam trains but I was glad to see the back of them, although we had no bother with leaves on the line as the heavier locos simply seemed to ride over them or the steam blew them away. In the main, however, steam engines were dirty, evil smelling horrors. Working at Laisterdyke Station on the Bradford to Leeds line was particularly bad as the Booking Office was immediately above the platforms and engine drivers seemed to delight in stopping and letting off clouds of steam and smoke, which permeated through the floorboards into the office, covering everything and everybody in dust and grime.

Laisterdyke was a very busy station with traffic from Crofts Engineering and English Electric; two very big firms. Not, however, as busy as Bradford Forster Square, which was an absolute hell hole with a never-ending mountain of parcels to dispatch, receive, sort, and enter on delivery sheets for the vanmen to distribute. This went on for 24 hours a day, every day of the year, including Christmas Day. I once worked seven Christmas Days in succession at Forster Square! My most vivid memory however was not concerned with the parcels at Forster Square but with the Booking Office. In my capacity as Station Relief Clerk I was always booked on for the Bank Holidays in the Booking Office and Easter Monday was always the busiest with many extra excursion trains.

This particular Easter Monday was very busy and I was booking the Wetherby Races Specials. Unknown to me, because I did not listen properly, there was a combined travel and admission to the racecourse ticket and also a travel only ticket for those who did not want to go to the races. In my ignorance I issued each passenger two tickets thinking that the combined ticket was for entry only. It was only when I ran out of travel tickets and asked for more that the error was discovered. Immediate panic! What had I done? The station concourse was heaving with passengers waiting to board the special trains and I was facing a loss of 250 tickets and a huge debit in hard cash! The Passenger Agent was spitting blood and I had a very definite feeling that at this moment in time I was not his favourite booking clerk.

He immediately ordered all spare station staff to go to the Wetherby platform and try and collect the travel tickets before the special train pulled in. The exercise was very successful as we collected nearly every ticket, including those that were genuine travel only tickets and I ended up with a big surplus in my balance. To this day I don't know how the passengers managed to travel back without a ticket, but we had no complaints. I was thereafter known as 'the two for the price of one clerk'!

Another incident happened at Bradford Forster Square in the days when refused perishable goods were allowed to be salvaged for the best available price to other traders, or as a last resort, to the staff at the best price possible. It was not uncommon for the consignee to refuse to accept late delivery traffic particularly at weekends when it would be more difficult to sell. The job of disposing the refused traffic fell to the Claims Clerk at Bradford Forster Square.

I remember one incident when a consignment of fish fillets dripping melting ice was refused on a Friday. No other fish merchant would accept and the Claims Clerk had to resort to selling to the staff. He set up his stall on a barrow on the station concourse. He began to trade but there was far too much fish and the staff were not all that interested. The general public however were and in no time he had a long queue of housewives buying his fish fillets. The circumstances were very amusing at the time and it was amazing where the people came from. The Claims Clerk ended up selling the fish at a higher price than the wholesale invoice price. This however was no surprise as it was something he invariably did when disposing of salvage to the staff. I certainly had my share of good and bad days but in general I always enjoyed my time with the railways and would be quite happy to do it all again.

SEMAPHORE SIGNALLING

Track Circuit: The principle of the track circuit is that the battery uses the rails as conductors to connect in a relay. A relay is basically a switch and is 'on when the track is clear'. When a trains wheels run over the rails they 'short out' the relay turning it off, which gives an indication in the signal box.

Station Limits: The portion of the line between the outermost home signal and the section signal (starter) for the same line, worked from the same signal box.

Absolute Block Section: From the section signal (starter) of a signal box to the outermost home signal of the box in advance.

Intermediate Block Section: The part of the line from the section signal (starter) to the same signal box's intermediate block home signal. This type of signalling is used to increase line capacity.

Permissive Block Working: Where more than one train at a time, travelling in the same direction could occupy a block section. Used on goods and slow lines.

Stop Signal: The arm is raised at an angle of 45 degrees to show clear and is described as an upper quadrant.

Distant Signal: In raised position, gives an indication to driver to proceed. In 'on position' (caution), informs driver to be prepared to stop at the next stop signal.

Junction Signals: Interlocking between the points and signals ensures the points are correctly set before the signals can be cleared.

Shunting Signals: Ground disc type. In off position: proceed, but only as far as line is clear.

Co-Acting Signal: A co-acting signal provides the driver with a long-range view of the signal (top arm) and a close range view (bottom arm).

Banner Repeater Signal: Banner repeater signals give a driver prior indication of the signal he is approaching to enable him to control his train efficiently. Used in locations where signal sighting is poor.

Subsidiary Signal: 'Calling On'. In off position: line towards next stop signal is occupied, proceed cautiously, and be prepared to stop short of any obstruction.

Subsidiary Signal: 'Shunt Ahead'. In off position: proceed forward cautiously for shunting purposes only.

WE'VE LOST THE PANTOGRAPH!

Derrick Boden

Driver, Derrick Boden rounds off 47 years of railway service
with a gift of a bottle of champagne

*The start of a career that was to span for 47 years for **Derrick Boden**, was at Belle Vue locomotive shed, Wakefield, in 1949. Derrick was just 16 years old and his first duties were as an engine cleaner. By far the worst aspect of this job, and usually given to the most junior persons, was to clean out the firebox after the fire had been dropped. This entailed climbing into the firebox after it had cooled down sufficiently, in order to clean the ashes off the brick arch, knock the clinkers off the ends of the smoke and super heater tubes and replace any missing or damaged fire bars. Sometimes the temperature in the firebox could be like working in an oven and even the air they were breathing was full of a glowing fine ash. Derrick was to spend seven years as a cleaner and passed cleaner before being promoted to fireman in 1956.*

There was an interval in this service when in April 1951 Derrick was called for National Service serving with the Oxford and Buckinghamshire Light Infantry in Cyprus and the Suez Canal

Zone of Egypt. There was an interesting sequel to his army service; on returning to Cowley Barracks, Oxford for his release, he noticed a young lady, who he found out was the Barrack Master's daughter. Derrick plucked up the courage to ask her out for a date and to his surprise she accepted. The date must have gone well for he and Pamela have now been married 47 happy years!

In 1966 Derrick took his locomotive driving test and was promoted to passed fireman, but shortly after, the Belle Vue shed closed. He moved on to Healey Mills Shed for the next ten years and then to Holbeck Shed as a registered driver in March 1977. In April 1986 his final move was to Leeds Station and based in the 'contract mileage link' driving HSTs and the InterCity 225s with the Class 91 Electric Locomotive between Newcastle and London King's Cross.

When based at Wakefield most of my early firing turns were on freight traffic on the Dearne Valley, calling at the collieries of Crofton, Grimethorpe, Goldthope and Rossington. We also worked into Lancashire calling at Rose Grove, Patricroft and Manchester Victoria. In the summer we used to work the passenger excursions to Blackpool, Scarborough and Cleethorpes. When some of the mill towns had their two weeks' holiday, the whole place would be virtually deserted as all the workers boarded the trains for a week at the seaside.

One Bank Holiday Monday I signed on duty as a spare man at 9am, not expecting to go very far. I was told I was working with a driver whose nickname was the 'Mighty Atom', with a Black Five engine to take a special excursion from Wakefield Kirkgate to Blackpool. Drawing into the platform at Kirkgate it was impossible to find a single space; there must have been over 600 passengers eager to get to the coast for a good day out. On arriving at our destination we were told the news: 'You are staying here to work the same train back'. We had not been married long and so I was worried that my wife would think there was something wrong when I was not home by teatime. Mighty Atom said; 'Don't worry, she will soon get used to this sort of thing and will realise that not only can you start duty any time of the day or night but it is never certain when you are finishing duty. It was after midnight when I finally arrived home and my wife had been really upset wondering what had happened to me. I gave her Mighty Atom's advice and told her never to worry again as I would always turn up eventually.

We got to know all the engines based at Kirkgate very well. There were good steamers and bad ones and they all had to be treated differently to get the best out of them. We used to work the Liverpool to Newcastle boat train for part of its journey and we used any one of three engines of the same class to do the job. All were completely different and had to be treated accordingly. No. 5698 *Mars* was a very temperamental beast and had to be coaxed along. No. 5717 *Dauntless* was by name and by nature a really bad steamer and one that train crews used to hate to work. The third, no. 5719 *Glorious* was a dream to work; we only had to show it the shovel and it was away. By the same yardstick there were drivers and drivers; some could make the fireman's job relatively easy while others as soon as they opened the regulator the engine would be dancing. We called them 'Tin Pot Charlie' or 'Heavy Handed Joe' and we never stopped shovelling.

You could say my apprenticeship to be a driver was about 17 years before I took my examination at York with Inspector Harry Potts. The examination took two days. During that time there was never any formal training. It was all down to yourself to pick things up from the driver you were with. We also had to learn the Rules and Regulations and there again these had to be learnt in our own time. There were Mutual Improvement Classes (MIC) and most firemen attended these at some time to gain the knowledge required in Rules and Regulations.

In 1977 on my move to Holbeck Shed as a fully registered driver, the variety of driving turns to different places was enormous. We could work to Liverpool, the Trans Pennines, York Expresses, Bangor Mail Train, Newspaper Trains, Freightliners, Coal Trains and jobs to Carlisle. On moving to Leeds Station in 1986 we could work to Birmingham, Derby, York, Newcastle, or London King's Cross and could be driving Deltics, Class 47 diesel locomotives, High Speed Trains and finally the InterCity 225 Class 91 Electric Locomotives.

I returned one evening on the 7.30pm London King's Cross to Leeds train of which, on this occasion, I was the assistant driver to a Doncaster man. We had just hurtled through Sandy at 125 miles per hour when everything on the locomotive went haywire. We eventually pulled up at Everton and went outside to discover that the pantograph had been ripped away and we had torn two miles of overhead wiring from its fixings. It was a Thursday evening and the East Coast Main Line was blocked until Sunday. The enquiry established it was a fault in the wiring and we were actually commended for carrying out the relevant safety procedures both on the locomotive and the track. On this occasion it was relatively easy to inform my wife I would be late home!

During my time, like most drivers I had plenty of scary moments but one that I will never forget was the day we were coming down Brodsworth Bank, Doncaster, with a type 40 locomotive and a full train of coal. We were only travelling at 5mph but the engine was not responding to the brakes and I knew we were in serious trouble. The second-man jumped off the loco to put sand on the rails to give the wheels something to grip on but to no avail. We went through the trap points and the locomotive left the rails and turned over on its side with me still at the controls. I considered myself very lucky to escape with my life in that incident. Having said that, if I had my time to do again, I would choose the same career.

MORE GOING LOCO

L. & Y. R. Radial Tank Class: First saw service in 1889. Designers: J A Aspinall and G Hughes. 20 survived into late 1950s.

F16 Class: Lancashire &Yorkshire 0-6-0 introduced in 1891. Mainly used on shunting duties.

G.W.R. 'City of Truro': One of a series of ten engines constructed in 1903. Recorded a speed of over 100mph in 1904.

N-1 class: Designed by H A Ivatt and came into service in 1907. A few survived at Leeds until the late 50s.

Castle Class: Introduced in 1923. One of the most successful locomotives ever built. Worked on the G.W.R. main line.

Lord Nelson Class 4-6-0: Introduced for the Southern Railway in 1926. Were employed between Waterloo, Southampton and Bournemouth.

King (60xx) Class: Originated on the G.W.R. in 1927. 6 ft 6 ins driving wheels. Employed on the Main lines Paddington to Plymouth and Bristol to Birmingham.

Condensing Pannier Tank Class 0-6-0PT: 1931. Specially adapted version fitted with condensing apparatus for tunnel working.

Stanier L.M.S. Mogul Class: Introduced in 1933. 5 ft 6 ins driving wheels. Used on fast heavy freight trains.

5-MT Class: Came into service in 1934 for the L.M.S. Comparable: To Jubilee Class. Only have two cylinders and smaller diameter driving wheels.

V-2 Class: Commenced service 1936 for L.N.E.R. Very few of this class carried names. Green Arrow (60800) was the first. Originally designed for fast freight.

Merchant Navy Class: Built for the Southern Railway and introduced in 1941. 6 ft 2 ins driving wheels. Produced by Bulleid and full of original ideas.

Q-1 Class: Introduced originally by G.C.R. 1942. 0-8-0- two of these engines were based at Selby.

Pacific A-2/3: First service 1943 by L.N.E.R. Subject to many modifications and rebuilds. Express passenger services between King's Cross and Aberdeen.

Pacific A1: Origin L.N.E.R. 1945. Fitted with smoke screens and double chimneys. Non-streamlined. Worked between King's Cross and Aberdeen.

THE BOSS IS HIDING ON PLATFORM 12

Gordon Ambler

'Normanton Lad' Gordon Ambler

Gordon Ambler and I have one great claim to fame: we were both born and raised in the West Yorkshire town of Normanton! Leaving school at 14 years, his first attempt at joining the railway was turned down through lack of height! His mother, being a single parent with five young mouths to feed, was desperate for Gordon to become a wage earner. Gordon was equally desperate to help out the financial hardship so he managed to persuade a local shop owner to take him on as a delivery boy with often-disastrous consequences. His second attempt at joining the railway was more successful, having grown the required height. His duties were as a steam locomotive cleaner at Normanton shed.

After gaining experience in firing duties, Gordon answered the immediate call for locomotive firemen in war-ravaged London. After many scary experiences and gaining experience he returned to the less stressful life of firing duties at his home depot of Normanton. However, the war now over he soon became bored with life in the small town and seeking some excitement in life, decided to leave the railways and join the army. He enlisted with the Royal Armoured Corps in April 1947 and was to serve for just short of six years, the majority of this time being spent in troubled Malaya due to the long running emergency and then with the post war British Army of the Rhine in Germany.

1953 saw him back on the now nationalised railway but this time working as a guard. Moving on to different locations as a shunter he eventually attained salaried status in 1964 as a Class 4 Inspector. With the added responsibility of a wife and two young children to support, Gordon moved to various locations around West Yorkshire, gaining experience in different grades and making steady promotional progress. In 1974 he made his last major move, as a supervisor to Leeds Station. He retired in 1992 as senior supervisor, having completed a total of 44 years service and for all the embarrassing moments, he still enjoyed the vast bulk of his time. In retirement Gordon is Treasurer of the Leeds Retired Staff Association.

I was born in Normanton in 1927 where I spent my childhood and school days. On leaving school at 14 years of age I decided that I would like to pursue a career on the railway. I made an application to the shed-master at Normanton and subsequently attended for an interview. My hopes were high but I was soon brought down to earth when I was informed that I was below the minimum height requirement. Although I was quite small and light of frame, I was quite fit and like lots of people my age, took part in many sporting activities.

I had to obtain some kind of employment and eventually became an errand boy delivering groceries on a custom built bicycle. The bicycle had an in-built frame at the front, which would take quite heavy loads. What a disaster that became! In those days, customers required enormous supplies of food for a week. Quite often I had to deliver 14lbs bags of flour (these being the days when housewives baked their bread in large quantities). The other male shop assistant would carry the loaded basket out to the bicycle and I straddled the brute ready to commence the journey.

After a dithering start I was on my way but much worse was to come. Having arrived at the place of delivery, I had to dismount which was easier said than done. Being my first delivery I was unsure how to stop. I didn't anticipate the somersaulting of the bike due to the heavy contents of the basket and the delivery was made to the pavement and not the house! This was not an everyday occurrence but it did happen frequently. I knew my employment was insecure due to my inability to stop the cycle safely with the groceries intact, and sure enough the manageress informed me that she would have to dispense with my services. I was to leave at the weekend.

The manageress was quite sympathetic; she could see my eyes were becoming moist. It wasn't so much to do with my job loss; it was because of the money my mother would miss being a single parent of five children. I only earned twelve shillings and sixpence per week (62½ pence). That was two shillings and sixpence (12½ pence) more than the benefit my mother received.

Saturday arrived, the day of my job termination. I could see the manageress was just as upset as I was. In desperation to keep my job I asked her if I could make two deliveries when there was an excessive load as there was quiet periods every day. To my relief, she agreed; we had arrived at an amicable situation. I continued with this job for nearly a year until I thought the time had arrived for me to make a further application to join the railway. This time I was successful and I became a cleaner at Normanton locomotive shed.

I was now among people of my own age in a different environment. The work was varied: cleaning steam locomotives, cleaning inner fireboxes and tubes. It was dirty work and we had no protective clothing. As a result we got very unpleasant skin irritations. Monotony became prevalent in most of us and all we could hope for was the coming of age (16) so that we could be passed out for firing duties. That day eventually arrived but even then when taking duty we never knew if we would be required to fire a steam locomotive or whether we would be back on cleaning duties. The days of 7:30am to 4pm had passed. I was now to work three shifts: early, late and night turns.

The initial period of firing duties to gain experience was at Normanton North and South marshalling yards. When we had gained this experience it was an exciting period going to stations and areas not seen previously. There was a downside in the relationship between driver and fireman. The generation gap was a feature that I didn't anticipate, and how much distance there would be between us. Our interests in life were totally different. The vast majority of drivers, being married with families naturally had different views and responsibilities in life. Nevertheless, it wasn't all doom and gloom and relationships improved as we became better acquainted.

There was an emergency situation in the London area. Firemen were in short supply and depots were asked to provide cover on a temporary basis. Several passed cleaners in West Yorkshire volunteered for these positions. I was one of them and we were accommodated in the Kentish Town Railway Hostel. The situation became so serious that we were on duty for extremely long hours. We were rolling in money but having no time to spend it. During this period bombs and the V1 and V2 rockets were unleashed upon London with intense fury. I, for one, made myself unavailable for duty on quite a few occasions and after a period of about six months, I returned back to my own depot; but it had been a very enlightening experience.

On returning to my job at Normanton I found that social life was at a minimum. Work and no play was difficult to endure so I tendered my resignation and enlisted in the army. I was to serve for just short of six years. There were good and bad times as in many walks of life: suffice it to say that I came out a much more wiser and responsible person; I had no regrets.

Back in civilian life I was looking through the local newspaper, and saw an advertisement for guards at the Ardsley Depot. I applied and was back working for the railway industry but this time at the rear of the train. Soon I realised that this was not for me. Boredom and loneliness were things I could not accept. People in large numbers had surrounded me for a long period in good times and bad. Solitude made me realise that I would be much happier if I was engaged in more activity. Scanning the vacancy list there was a position for a shunter at Normanton. My application was accepted. Here began a new chapter in my life.

Life was never dull in the shunting yards of Normanton. The place had its fair share of characters, one of whom was called Bert. He had the reputation of being able to tell a few 'porky pies'. One of his shunting colleagues had noticed a furniture van at Bert's house and the men removing a piano and taking it away. 'What's up Bert? Have you fallen behind with your payments again?' 'No', came the reply, 'I've sent the piano back, because it plays two tunes at the same time'! On another occasion in the shunters cabin, the men were discussing the television programmes of the previous night. Bert chipped in his two penn'orth: 'Best viewing I've ever seen'. One of the men said to him: 'How do you know? You haven't got a television. In fact you don't have electricity'. Bert replied, 'You don't necessarily have to have electricity; I have just bought a 'gas set'. The only difference is, the screen is blue!'

One day on the 6.0am to 2.0pm turn the Inspector told me I was wanted on the phone by the roster clerk. I was asked if I would work until 6.0pm as someone had rung in sick. Glad of the overtime, I said yes. My brother lived near the station, so I called at his home for a 'cuppa and a sarnie' and returned to take up my duties from 2.0pm until 6.0pm. I was told that a full team was on duty and suddenly realised that someone had played a trick on me, imitating the roster clerk's voice. I was told it was the 'yard signalman' who had played the prank, so I thought I would have my revenge. While the signalman was on the early turn I rang him and said his relief was unable to take duty, so would he stay till 6.0pm? 'I can't do that' he said, 'who's speaking?' I replied 'Inspector Jardine' who was the signalling inspector. He replied, 'For your information, Inspector Jardine is a Scotsman and doesn't speak with a West Yorkshire accent'. Result: Played 2 Lost 2.

I eventually had some success even if there were a few obstacles in my way. Redundancies were inevitable with new marshalling yards being introduced at Stourton and Healey Mills. Last in, first out, I was on my way to the latter. Now working at Healey Mills once again I was on strange ground. I now had responsibilities, a wife and two children; there was no other alternative. The inspector at the west end of the yard didn't seem too pleased with my arrival. In fact, he doubted my abilities. 'I've just lost the best senior rail man at this yard'; 'Well now you've got a better one' I replied. He walked away mumbling obscenities. The stationmaster gave me two weeks to acquaint myself with the geographical layout of the yard and I made the best of it. Training over, I was now committed to show the doubting inspector of what I had been doing for the last three years. He must have been pleased with my performance for we became the best of friends. I attended movement and signalling classes and that proved to have the desired effect for promotional prospect.

The remainder of my career was in the salaried grades holding several positions for 28 years. On one occasion there was a disturbance at the Leeds ticket barriers; I at the time was the station supervisor. There was an alarm system from the barrier to the supervisor's office. The alarm sounded so I attended the ticket barrier to see what the problem was. A British Transport Policeman was attempting to arrest a man who had consumed a large amount of fighting alcohol. The situation became more explosive as the culprit had two brothers who were intent on releasing the policeman's hold on their brother. The officer held the offender in an arm lock and who, when I approached him to tell him to calm down, attempted to kick me in the groin. The attempt failed, as I was able to step back and then deliver the same treatment in the same region with great success. The policeman said to me; 'You could be in serious trouble as that amounts to assault'! 'I know' I replied, 'But my wedding tackle is still intact'.

It was Saturday night at Leeds Station. The last passenger train had departed; all was quiet. Suddenly, the sound of bagpipes filled the air, emanating from the overhead staff barrow crossing. Enter the boss on his nightly rounds; he wasn't best pleased at the wailing sound and ordered me to bring the offender to his office. I ushered the railman in and was just leaving when the boss said; 'Stay here and listen to what I have to say to him'. The rebuking commenced, saliva was on his lips and the offender was treated to a shower as well as a good cursing. 'You have applied to become a sleeping car attendant haven't you?' 'Yes' replied the wailing piper. 'Well you're not going to have that pleasure', said the boss, 'we don't put wailing pipers on sleeping car trains'!

On another occasion I was called to a suicidal situation. On arrival the engine driver told me a man had jumped in front of his train but didn't know if he was dead or alive. It was a dark gloomy night and I had difficulty in locating the person, looking under the train wagons with just the glow of my paraffin hand lamp. I was extremely nervous of what I would find, as it was a first-time experience of this nature for me but one as a supervisor I had to carry out. Eventually I located him lying between the rails in a terrified state and unable to move. I crawled under the vehicle to see if he had any injuries but apart from a few scratches and bruises he was, amazingly, in one piece. After talking to him for a few minutes I was able to assist him from under the train to a place of safety. After a while he regained his composure and told me the reason he wanted to end his life. He was a student at Leeds University, residing with three others. He was much slower in his studies and unable to keep up with the others due to having been struck on the head by a golf ball when a youngster. This in turn caused him to suffer from blackouts with the result he became really depressed. I did my best to talk him round and said he should study at his own pace and not worry about the others. I never knew what became of him but I sincerely hope he achieved his ambitions.

My most embarrassing moment was again at Leeds Station when duty supervisor. A severe points failure had brought the station to a halt and chaos reigned supreme. To make matters worse it was the evening rush hour with thousands of passengers anxious to be on their way home. In my office I was being bombarded with questions I could not answer from very irate passengers. One male passenger was shouting at me and calling me names that were not on my birth certificate. A large crowd was now gathered round my desk. The main complainant was persistent in giving me a lot of grief and demanded I get hold of the man in charge of the station to his presence. My reply was: 'It's not a man, it's a woman by the name of Heidi and she's hiding on platform 12'. I immediately looked up at the angry crowd for their reaction to that little gem and to my horror saw that Heidi, the boss, was among them! I just wanted to crawl into a hole in the ground. For all that I really did enjoy my railway career and the good times far outweighed the bad and indeed embarrassing moments.

BY THE LAY BY

1841: The railway detonator invented by Mr E.A. Cowper.

1861: First interlocked signal box. Oakenshaw Junction.

1866: First engineering weekly notices.

1876: The first track circuit installed at Crystal Palace, following its invention in the USA in 1872.

1878: Audible fog signals tried on Enfield branch.

1879: Petroleum replaces candles.

1894: First track circuits introduced. King's Cross.

1900: Disc signals introduced.

1910: Rotary block introduced.

1920: First colour light signals.

1928: Upper quadrant signals. LMS.

1934: Standard ground disc signals.

1952: Telegraph bell replaced by goods block instrument.

I'M IN CHARGE

Paul Opresco

All Aboard with Senior Conductor, Paul Opresco

*I was just 12 years old when I first came to know **Paul Opresco**. At that time my main interest in life above all others was playing football. It so happened that a man with an unusual accent had come to live quite near my family. He was an excellent footballer and willing to give me tips to improve my play. His name was Paul Opresco. Born in Overton, Hampshire, in 1922, he moved with his family to Guildford Surrey at the age of 14 years. His first job was as an apprentice Rate Fixer for the heavy vehicle manufacturers: Dennis. In 1935 he joined the Queen's Royal Regiment (Territorial) as a boy soldier. At the outbreak of the Second World War he was called to serve with the regular battalion, seeing action in Algeria and Tunisia with the First Army. In 1942 he was transferred to the Royal Electrical and Mechanical Engineers and took part in the whole of the bloody Italian campaign, in continuous action until the end of hostilities. On demobilisation in 1946 Paul married a Normanton girl, Phyllis, and they recently celebrated their 56th wedding anniversary.*

Paul's railway career began at Crofton Junction in 1947 when he became a shunter. He then moved to Wakefield Kirkgate loco shed as a cleaner and later as a fireman. After several years he decided to try something different and for the next four years was a coal miner employed at Normanton Newland Colliery. He left the mine for health reasons and returned to his old job as shunter at Crofton Junction and then transferred to be a freight guard, which he found he enjoyed immensely. On his 49th birthday he transferred to Leeds as a passenger guard and gained promotion to conductor guard from which position he retired in 1987 having notched up 36 years enjoyable service. A likeable man, throughout his career, Paul would always go out of his way to help a colleague or a passenger, an excellent railwayman.

On the 29th April 1973 I was the guard working the 13.25 Bradford to Sheffield diesel multiple unit passenger train. The journey was just normal routine until we arrived at South Kirkby Junction where the signals were at red. After a time my driver went on the phone, to be told that the reason for the delay was that there was a track circuit failure and we were awaiting a signal fitter being called out. Having previous experience of working in and out of South Kirkby Colliery as a freight guard I knew where the necessary equipment was to enable me, if required, to switch the points. I informed the Control Office that I could switch the points and so enable my train to clear the junction so the Leeds to London King's Cross train behind us would not be delayed. They immediately said if I could do the job it would save a lot of delay. I clipped and scotched the points so allowing my train to proceed onto the branch to a safe distance. I then returned the points to the main line position so allowing the Leeds to King's Cross train to continue its journey without delay. I then rejoined my train to continue our journey to Sheffield knowing that I had saved a lot of inconvenience to hundreds of passengers. I subsequently received a letter from my Area Manager, thanking me for my actions.

On another occasion, 8th November 1980, I was the guard working the 10.50 King's Cross to Leeds service. I was fortunate that travelling back on this service were several Leeds guards who had worked special trains to King's Cross in preparation for the Armistice Day Parade. Most of the passengers on this train were Arsenal supporters who were to watch their team play Leeds United. All was well till we departed our last stop Wakefield Westgate, where Leeds United fans joined the train.

Within minutes fighting broke out and I was directed to a young man with a knife wound. I informed the driver who stopped at the next signal and requested sufficient police to meet the train and an ambulance for the injured person. I then requested the assistance of the spare guards and told them to lock all the doors of the train so on arrival at Leeds Station the police could board and detain the main culprits. I was also in luck because a policeman had joined the train at Wakefield and he had been able to arrest the man suspected of committing the stabbing. To their credit, most of the Arsenal fans actually apologised to me for some of their colleagues' behaviour. It was all in a day's work and the exception to the rule as most journeys were without these types of incident.

THE SENIOR CONDUCTOR

It's four in the morning, the alarm it does ring,
It's time to get up before the birds even sing.
Have a wash and a shave, now that feels just fine,
Make the tea and the toast, give my shoes a quick shine.

Bike out of the shed, must arrive work on time,
Sign on at the window, it's now half past five.
The roster clerk says 'here shake a leg'
This is your workings, go down to the shed.

The train is in darkness, it's cold and it's damp,
I've got to prepare it ; now where's my hand lamp?
I first check the outside,the couplings and pipes,
Check doors and the windows, the head and tail lights.

When all is in order, inside I climb,
I look at my watch, I'm still in good time.
I check all the seating and up on the racks,
How clean are the carpets? Check the vestibule mats.

Now check all the toilets and water tanks too,
Soap and handtowels, and the flush of the loo,
The brake test completed, tell the driver the load,
The speed of the slowest, any privately owned.

It's right away driver, to the station we go,
The signals are yellows along the up slow.
The reservations all slotted onto the seat backs,
Quick check with control all's clear on the tracks.

Our customers join us, impatient I know,
Pre - departure announcement, receive tip to go.
Give two on the bell, have a last look about,
Must stay at the window for alarm signs or shout.

'Good morning Ladies and Gentlemen', now everything is fine,
We're travelling to London and making good time,
Count all the customers: How many have we got?
Report on the POIS form any defects I spot.

Now to check tickets a job I must do,
I check everybody, yes, including the loo.
Someone without one, no problem at all
Credit card, cash, cheque: I take them all.

The restaurant is busy, a truly wonderful smell,
The great British breakfast, I know it so well.
The steward, the waiters are dashing about,
The countryside passing as the diners look out.

As King's Cross draws near, it's the end of the line,
A quick check on my watch, yes, we've arrived there on time.
On behalf of the train crew I'm pleased to say
Thank you for travelling InterCity today!

P.K.

MORE OF THE WORLD OUTSIDE

1970-75: Steep rise in oil prices, 1973, produced recession in Western Europe and USA (e.g. 25% inflation in Britain in 1975). Era of the 'silicon chip', increasing use of computers in offices and factories.

1975-79: Closer relationship between Catholic and Protestant Churches, but signs of religious decline in many Western countries. Cinema in the West in popular decline due to television and video competition. Fertility drugs and 'test-tube baby' techniques developed.

1980-89: Prince and Princess of Wales married, 1981. Thatcher government organises successful military and naval campaign to expel Argentine forces from Falkland Islands, 1982. Thatcher also defeats miners' strike, 1984-5 and curbs trade-union powers. Building of Channel Tunnel between Britain and France begun, 1986.

1990-95: Collapse of communism in Soviet Union led to Gorbachev's resignation, December 1991. Destruction of ozone layer causing concern: attempts to address this problem at international 'Earth Summit' in Rio de Janerio, 1992. Massive oil resources in seas of South Antarctic (off Falkland Islands) found, 1993. Official opening of Channel Tunnel, May 1994. Argentina and Britain agree on joint oil exploration, 1995.

A TALE OF TWO CATS?

Andy Stephenson

A smart looking Andy Stephenson at a well presented
Appleby Station, on the Settle - Carlisle line

*With a famous surname like his it was no wonder **Andrew (Andy) Stephenson** was to join the railway. His grandfather worked as a drayman on the LMS Railway at Leeds. Memories of Andy when we worked in the commercial department were of a man who enjoyed his work and was dedicated to the job. Whatever the crisis he was one of the few who would always greet people with a smile and have a calming influence on the situation. Andy joined the service in June 1958 and was to complete 39 years service in the clerical and managerial grades. His first post was as a junior clerk in the goods office at Stanningley. He then went on to work at various local stations until in 1960 he moved to the Divisional Manager's Office, Leeds, working in both commercial and operating departments. In 1984 he moved to the Area Manager's Office, Leeds, as Head of Customer Services. His final move was to the York Headquarters where he was Head of Technical Services until retirement in 1997. In retirement he is now able to pursue his hobbies of travelling, walking and reading.*

In 1960 I was working in the Coach Rolling Stock Section of the Divisional Managers Office, Leeds. This section had a number of inspectors who travelled out and about to check on the maintenance of the rolling stock. One of these inspectors was called Ted Stubbs. Ted was always laid back, did not panic, and always had a smile on his face, but I was assured that in an emergency, Ted was your man. One Friday at 4.10pm, the day before the Rugby League Cup Final a call came from Bradford Forster Square saying they had just started tanking (filling the coach toilets with water) the special trains being used for the Cup Final and they had found a number of bursts: 'What were they to do?' 'I'll get an inspector out as soon as possible' said the boss. But on replacing the phone he realised that the inspectors finished duty at 4.0pm. Just then, the office door opened and in rushed Ted, running late and eager to be home.

'Quick' said the boss, 'get out to Forster Square; there's a crisis with the stock for the Cup Final tomorrow'. Being new to the job I thought, now I am going to see how an expert deals with a crisis; I'll definitely learn something here. Ted, on receiving the command did not panic but immediately leapt for the phone. 'Is that Shipley station?' asked Ted; 'right, the 4.21 arrival from Leeds will be with you in a few minutes. Wilf Gray the coaching stock inspector will be getting off that train on his way home. Tell him to stay on the train and go through to Forster Square as he is wanted there to sort out a crisis!' With that Ted put the phone down, looked at us all open mouthed and said; 'Right that's sorted I'm off home', and off he went. I must admit I never saw another crisis resolved as quick during the rest of my career.

Two booking clerks were working the late shift at Shipley Booking Office in the late 1960s. They were being plagued by the incessant cries of a cat in a box that had been brought in earlier that day to go on the evening parcel train to Bristol. (In those days livestock was sent by rail unaccompanied.) On examining the label they discovered it was a pedigree cat to be collected at Bristol the following morning. The clerks decided the cat was complaining about the indignity of being locked up and that if they let it out in the secure office it would shut up. They released the pedigree cat into the office where it was free to roam about, and peace once again prevailed. After a while one of the clerks needed to use the toilet, which was outside the office. Due care was taken when he left the room to ensure the cat did not escape. Unfortunately on his return he had forgotten about the cat and as he opened the door it shot out of the office and down the platform.

The clerks spent the next 30 minutes desperately searching the station for the purebred feline. They returned empty-handed to await the severe reprimand they would surely get next day. Suddenly they heard a cat crying at the door and thought salvation was at hand. This was short lived as on opening the door they discovered it was the mangy station cat. This had appeared about six months earlier as a stray. They had taken pity on it and fed it and since then it had adopted the station. Both clerks had the same idea at once. The scruffy station cat suddenly received for the first time in its life a careful wash and brush-up. Placed into the empty cat-box it departed on the parcels train for a new life of pampered luxury. Both clerks were pretty anxious for the following few days, but no complaints from Bristol were ever received. The fate of the unfortunate pedigree cat was never known.

A queue had developed at the booking office window at Bradford. One of the early turn clerks had called in sick. Another clerk appeared and started opening the second window. This was the late turn clerk who had come in early on overtime to relieve the situation. Suddenly an annoyed voice erupted from the back of the queue and shouted: 'This is ridiculous, get yourself sorted out, after all we pay your wages'. Quick as a flash the new clerk shouted back. 'I've been looking for you, I'm not standing here and taking all this abuse for the paltry wages you pay me; I want an increase in pay'! The man at the back of the queue was shocked by this response and said: 'I'm going to Leeds to buy a ticket' and quickly departed. He was never seen again.

A young man employed in customer services failed to report for work on the Monday following his two weeks annual leave. Nothing was heard from him for the reason of his absence. Next day when he came in to work I informed him that he had to report to the personnel manager. He duly appeared in front of the manager. 'Right, you know the rule, you must advise your head of section if you are unable to take duty. Why didn't you ring in yesterday?' 'I was laid up in bed all day and couldn't get to a phone' was the response. 'What was wrong with you?' enquired the manager. 'Jet-lag' was the reply. 'Where did you go on your holiday?' asked the manager in surprise. 'Benidorm' was the reply!

While I was in charge of customer services at Leeds one of the clerks had got involved in a private venture with one of the operating inspectors, running charter trains on a weekend. One day the inspector came to see me and said would it be all right if the clerk accompanied him while they nipped to the bank, as both signatures were required in connection with running the charter trains that weekend. I thought as it was of benefit to the railway I agreed. Two hours later the clerk returned. I challenged him; 'Where have you been, it doesn't take two hours to nip to the bank?' 'Yes it does' he said: 'We bank in Barnsley!

A manager who dealt with matters regarding ASLEF and the NUR related this story to me. One day he received a letter from the Line Secretary at York. This informed him that the Healey Mills loco were disputing the walking time they were allowed from the signing on point at Wakefield Kirkgate to the stabling sidings. The manager rang the Line Secretary and it was agreed they would have a site meeting one Saturday with the Local Departmental Committee (LDC) when they would walk between the two points to time the distance exactly. When the Saturday arrived for the meeting, there was a steady downpour of rain. The ASLEF representative took the manager to one side and said: 'We don't want to be walking outside in this weather; let's go to the pub for a hour and see if it stops'.

Everyone went to the pub but by 12 noon the weather was no better. 'Look', said the ASLEF rep, 'Lets not bother doing the walk in this atrocious weather'. 'That's OK', said the manager, 'but I have to report back on the outcome of the meeting'. The rep said, 'tell them we have walked the route and your assessment of the time is agreed. I will let you have a letter confirming this in a few weeks' time'. The weather was now really bad so they stayed in the pub until 3.0pm when the landlord announced it was closing time. When they made their way to the door the rain was even worse, with a cloudburst. 'Come on' said the landlord, 'Let's have you out'. They protested that they had been in the pub for four hours and in the process spent a fortune 'so you should let us stay until the rain eases'. 'It's closing time', said the landlord and pushed them out into the rain, closing the door behind them. A few weeks later the manager received a letter from the line secretary saying that as they had been unable to resolve the issue of walking time, another site meeting had to be arranged.

During my time at the Area Manager's Office, Leeds, there were numerous management meetings where a buffet was provided. One of the female secretaries had recommended her brother's catering business to provide the buffets. All went well until after one particular meal, some of the managers who had eaten the buffet were ill with food poisoning. The British Rail Medical Officer at York was contacted and arrangements were made for all those affected to supply a sample of their stools for tests. They would also contact the Health Authority who would visit the catering premises. Rumour had it that the secretary got wind of the impending visit and tipped her brother off in advance. Ever after that, she was nicknamed, 'The Stool Pigeon'!

THE GREAT BRITISH PUBLIC

Customer: What time is the next train to Leeds?
Clerk: 1.13.
Customer: Is there one before that?

Customer: What time is the last train from Leeds?
Clerk: 23.15.
Customer: Is there one after that.

Customer: Halifax please.
Clerk: Single or return?
Customer: Which is the cheapest.

Customer: I bought these tickets here yesterday and I'm concerned
       I'm not going to get any disabled assistance.
Clerk: I'll just check the forms have been made out and sent off.
    You
     did ask for assistance?
Customer: No.

Customer: Can I have a super advance on the 1505 Leeds to King's
       Cross tomorrow please?
Clerk: Sorry, none available.
Customer: What about the 1605?
Clerk: No, nothing until the 1805.
Customer: What about the 1705?
Clerk: No, I've just said, nothing until the 1805.
Customer: How about earlier?
Clerk: What do you mean by earlier?
Customer: What about the 1505?

Man: Was there a train due to arrive at Leeds from Bristol at 17.00?

Clerk: Yes.

Man: Did it arrive on time?

Clerk: Yes.

Man: So anyone getting off that train should have got to Hunslet (a Leeds Suburb) by now, 1930?

Clerk: Yes.

Man: Oh well, never mind, it was only the mother-in-law!

Clerk: Having just sold a youth a ticket to Sheffield

Youth: I have just had a look at the information screen and for the Sheffield train it says 'bus'. Does this mean it's a busy train?

Old lady: My son is travelling from Doncaster and he's over a hour late, are there any delays?

Clerk: Yes, there's been a fatality at South Elmsall earlier, so all trains are running a hour late.

Old lady: Oh dear, I hope nobody was hurt!

DRINKING ON DUTY?

Shirley Mitchell
(Donald's wife)

Retired driver, Donald Mitchell in holiday mode

Donald Mitchell *commenced his career at Copley Hill engine shed in 1946. Starting as an engine cleaner he progressed to fireman and driver and in doing so moved to Holbeck shed and ended his career based at Leeds Station. Donald had served the railways for 49 years when he retired in July 1995. Unfortunately he was to enjoy only four years of retirement before he died. His wife, Shirley, tells the following story, which goes back some 44 years and in the days when Driver and Fireman did full day trips.*

I went with Donald on a day trip to Cleethorpes. On the way home we were stopped outside Leeds Station by signals. All the passengers were stood in the isles and the lady in front of me was grumbling about having to wait. Then all of a sudden, she said in a loud voice; 'I bet the driver and fireman have gone to the pub for a drink while we are stood here!' Before I could stop myself, I tapped her on the shoulder and said to her, 'That is my husband you are talking about and for your information he doesn't drink when on duty and as you can see, I have a young baby with me and he knows I want to get her home to bed'. The lady went blood red and her husband turned to her and said; 'When are you going to learn to keep your big mouth shut'. The woman could not get away from me quickly enough, once the train had pulled into the station!

171

CONVEYANCE OF PASSENGERS

The range of fares offered by the railway companies are complex and often difficult for the general public to understand. From the very conception of passenger travel a wide range of fares was applicable for the same journey from A to B. Class of travel, type of train, difference in route, time of day were all factors that played a part in determining the fare to be paid. Social considerations and concessions grew to cover differing sections of the community. The police, armed forces and workmen's tickets were soon introduced along with early type season tickets for the every day user. The Cheap Trains Act empowered the Railway Commissioners to insist upon adequate accommodation for workmen going to and from their place of toil at such fares and at such times, as deemed to be reasonable and necessary.

Accompanied animals and articles was another form of revenue earning for the railway companies. Many passengers travelling on reduced cheap fares were not allowed any free luggage allowance at all. But for longer journeys luggage was an accepted part of the contract and the usual weight allowance was 150 lbs for first class passengers and 100 lbs for those travelling third class. Animals of all shapes and sizes were transported but to comply with safety regulations any considered dangerous or harmful were transported in the guard's van or in special vehicles. Many breeds of large dogs had to be muzzled and travel in the guard's van. Small animals could accompany their owner but had to remain on the floor and were not allowed on passenger seating.

Many passengers wanted to leave articles at the station for later collection, which brought about the introduction of the Left Luggage Office. They also invariably offered cloakroom facilities and also became the Lost property Office. This in itself turned out to be a substantial business as a surprising volume of lost property handed in was never reclaimed. Each railway company on a regular basis held regular sales of these goods and commodities. To help passengers going on holiday and save them the trauma of carrying heavy suitcases a Passengers' Luggage in Advance scheme was introduced. The luggage would be collected by motor transport and delivered to the passengers' destination so they could enjoy a relaxed hassle-free journey. This also saved the traveller the problem of whether to give the porter a tip for carrying their luggage. Officially porters were not to accept gratuities but it became accepted by and large for the travelling public to give a small tip. Most medium and large stations had ticket barriers to control entrance and exit to the platforms. People not travelling but wishing to gain access to the platforms could purchase a penny platform ticket from the red platform ticket machine usually placed adjacent to the ticket barriers. The first platform ticket machine was installed at Chippenham station on the Great Western Railway in 1912.

So, from the humble beginnings of transporting passengers, hundreds of jobs evolved and few people were not touched by the railways in one way or another. By 1900 the workforce had expanded to 400,000 employees directly and thousands more employed in providing services or supplies. The age of the train had arrived!

A STIFF IN THE LOO

John Harrison

Those boots were made for walking:
Retired BTC Police Inspector - John Harrison

John Harrison left school in 1960 to serve an apprenticeship as a coach painter and sign writer at Crewe Locomotive Works. He had no previous connections with the industry but he did eventually marry into a railway family. Having completed his apprenticeship John decided he would like to try for a life of more excitement. One of his workmates suggested he try for the fire service or the police force. Taking the plunge he applied for and was accepted into the Cheshire Police Force commencing in 1966. Having witnessed first hand how the British Transport Police operated he decided in 1977 to transfer his allegiance to the Railway 'Bobbies'. John took promotion as a dog handler as a Sergeant at Carlisle Citadel Station in 1977 and then moved on promotion to Inspector at Leeds Station in 1982. John took early retirement in 1996 after completing 32 years' service. In retirement his favourite hobby is walking the Dales, Peak District and Scotland.

Having duly served an apprenticeship in Crewe Locomotive Works, life as a police officer tends not to enter one's head, but it's a funny old world. In my early twenties, seeking something further out of life, a challenge of some sort, I decided to try for the police force. After passing the medical and entrance examinations I completed the training course and became a member of the Cheshire Police Force.

Some few months into my service and still a probationary constable I was on foot patrol in Crewe town centre. We had just been equipped with the latest radio technology when it suddenly came to life. I was to attend Crewe Railway Station as a body had been discovered in one of the toilets! Come-on, I thought: someone is having a bit of fun at my expense, this is a wind-up, so I continued on my patrol. The peace was once again shattered when my radio barked into life with a rather irate duty sergeant who informed me in no uncertain terms that it definitely was not a wind-up and that I should liaise with the British Transport Police on arrival at the station. On arrival, a female BTP officer escorted me to the male staff toilets. I was duly advised of the male personage sat in 'trap 3' (her words not mine). On peering under the door, was a male sat in the appropriate position, trousers around ankles. Suffice to say that, after death being confirmed and the body removed, the paper work commenced (no pun intended) and it was later confirmed that the poor chap had died of natural causes. This was the first case I had dealt with as a joint enquiry with the BTP and I was impressed, not only with the efficiency on this occasion but the compassion and integrity that was obviously required when dealing with the deceased's relatives.

A couple of years later I found myself transferring to the BTP, due to the fact that the then Cheshire Police tried to push their younger officers into police authority-owned accommodation and would not allow one to live in one's own house (albeit with a mortgage). So the wheel turned full circle so to speak and I was back working on the railway. Police Forces around the country lost a lot of officers in the late 60s early 70s because of their archaic housing policy but that is another story.

As a police officer on the railway you often found yourself working on your own, as there were not the same manning levels as in the civil police. I personally found it advantageous, as you were one of their community, both rail and postal staff at stations and depots worked closely together; they had to if the work was to achieve a satisfactory result. Far from being a lone PC, I felt privileged to be accepted as part of a huge family organisation. In fact both rail and postal staff came to my assistance on occasions when required and it was not just to pick my helmet up, or elevate me from the horizontal position where a drunk/thief/football hooligan (sometimes all three) had positioned me!

Some 18 months into my service with the BT Police, my Inspector asked me about my thoughts with regard to my career development and had I considered the dog section? A few months later saw me on a 13-week dog-training course at the Force Dog Training School at Elstree in Hertfordshire. The school was run by a man known to all and sundry as The Guv'nor. He believed in teaching by example, which some may consider unorthodox (but effective) by today's standards. One day I and my dog were on a training exercise known as the 'search for the hidden criminal'. We were in woodland when my dog, working loose about 70 yards ahead, indicated a find by barking, so I raised my hand to the kennel staff instructor and went forward to join my dog and 'arrest' the criminal. On reaching the place, I initially could not see what the dog had been barking at and wrongly assumed the dog had become distracted from his task and had chased a squirrel up a tree. Somewhat annoyed I (wrongly) bent down to take my dog by the scruff of the neck to chastise him for taking me on a false trail. Suddenly I was hit behind the head, knocking me off balance. As I recovered, I looked up to see The Guv'nor dropping out of the said tree, imparting words to the effect: 'You were wrong; your dog was right. My stick could have been an iron bar. Learn to trust your dog'. From that day I trusted my dog implicitly (most of the time)!

March 1972 if my memory serves correct, saw my dog Nikki and I as part of a serial of officers, escorting a train containing about 480 soccer fans from Stoke City to Wembley for the League Cup Final against, I think, Chelsea. (We are not talking a lot of officers: it was a Sergeant and four Constables with yours truly and dog.) However, on this occasion there was little trouble, plenty of banter with the fans and the day was going well. As we were approaching Wembley, I proceeded to walk the length of the train as usual so as to be in the front coach ready for disembarkation. Now this well-trained police dog is walking through the Tourist Second Open (TSO) coach (middle aisle, four seat tables on either side). The fans were eating, drinking (yes, beer cans were allowed then), when about halfway along the coach I noticed my dog lift his head, as a chap was holding this pork pie in his hand, elbow on arm rest, pie and hand dangling outwards towards aisle. He had his back to the dog and me. The scene suddenly went into slow motion as I realised what was about to happen and failed to react before my dog. Too late, I shouted 'Leave!' One pork pie was gratefully (and yes gracefully) received by one hungry dog. The coach erupted, at my expense, my (red) face must have told it all as I attempted to apologise to the late owner of said pork pie, who, fortunately, as did his mates, took the incident in good part. One unforgettable football special, but for me, for the wrong reason.

CLICKETY-CLICK

In the days of jointed track it was quite easy to work out a train's speed. If there were 22 clickety-clicks in 15 seconds, we were doing 60mph. 90 mph was 33 clickety-clicks in 15 seconds but 120 mph running (44 clickety-clicks in 15 seconds) probably never occurred because such speeds required welded rails – and no clickety-clicks. *

Another way was to time a train as it passed the mile, three-quarter-mile, half-mile and quarter-mile posts. If it took 15 seconds to do a quarter of a mile, we were doing 60mph. Likewise a quarter of a mile at 90 mph takes 10 seconds, and at 120 mph 7½ seconds. The continued existence of mileposts makes it possible to make a good estimate of speeds, although preferably over longer time periods than a quarter of a minute. For example, a train doing 125 mph will cover five miles in two minutes and 24 seconds. Trouble is that at that speed the mileposts pass in a bit of a haze.

We owe the existence of the mileposts to the Railways Clauses Act of 1845. The Act compelled all railway companies to erect mile, three-quarter-mile, half-mile and quarter-mile posts along all their lines. All the measurements had to start somewhere and this was either a junction or a station.

The North Eastern Railway, for example, carried out a re-miling exercise, which was concluded in 1905. The cast iron posts that can still be seen on all ex-NER lines date from this time. The exact start of the NER's measurements was marked by a Zero Post. The present York station, opened in 1877, was the start of the measurements of seven main lines of varying lengths - York to Newcastle, Normanton, Scarborough, Harrogate and Market Weighton, Market Weighton to Beverley, and Church Fenton to Micklefield – as well as three short lines at Northallerton, Pilmoor and Sherburn (in-Elmet). (There are plans to restore York's long-lost Zero Post.)

* 60 feet = 20 yards. There are 88 x 20 yards in a mile. 60 mph is a mile in 60 seconds, or 88 clickety-clicks. Therefore there are 22 clickety-clicks in 15 seconds.

YOU BOY, YOU WILL CLEAN THE WAITING ROOM

Ronnie Stead

From Junior Porter to Station Manager
Ronnie Stead with railman Norman Buckley 1984

I have known **Ronnie Stead** *as a colleague and friend for over thirty years. Although I never worked with him directly, I did once have to strike a deal with him, all in the line of duty. It happened in about 1985, when I was in charge of a team of ticket inspectors. Our accommodation in what was known as the 'Crows Nest' situated in the Parcels Concentration Depot (PCD) at Leeds City station was being demolished, as it was well past its sell by date. I was desperate to find some decent accommodation for the team and eventually found some vacant offices adjacent to the Power Signal Box above the station. I contacted Mr Ronnie Stead, Station Manager, about the availability of this accommodation. He said: 'I'll come and see you in a couple of days' time'. Ronnie came to my office, sat down and his gaze caught the sight of the very old railway clock ticking away on the wall. He said: 'You can have those offices subject to one condition?'. 'What's that?' I replied. He said: 'If you let me have that clock on the wall'. The deal was done and to this day Ronnie still reminds me that I no longer have the offices but he still has the clock!*

179

Ronnie was always a popular boss with the staff, and always looked after their welfare. However, he did not suffer fools gladly. I witnessed one or two employees receive the sharp end of his tongue, but they never came back for a second helping. His career started just months after the country had earned a reprieve by winning the Battle of Britain and never again would there be a time when the running of the railways would play such an important part in the nation's salvation. Commencing on the 3rd February 1941 as a telegraph messenger lad at Leeds City Station with the LMS, he moved on to be a porter, followed by a stint as a goods guard. He eventually gained promotion to a foreman before promotion to the supervisory grade by becoming a yard inspector. He then became a passenger yard inspector and then moved into the parcels department. He became a traffic assistant followed by spells at Leeds and York as Assistant Station Manager. Moving to Harrogate as Station Manager, his last appointment was to the position of Station Manager, Leeds. Ronnie poses the question: 'How many people can say they started at the lowest position at a station and finished up at the highest at the same station?' Well, Ronnie can, for that is what he achieved. On his last day of doing the rounds at Leeds Station: Ronnie had completed 47 years and 347 days. In retirement his hobbies are gardening, reading and extensive travelling, seeing as much of the world as possible.

I commenced my career with the L.M.S. on 3rd February 1941 at Leeds Station. My designation was Junior Porter Telegraph Messenger. At the same time two other lads started with me and they were Junior Clerk Telegraph Messengers. When the Chief Clerk interviewed us all I was made immediately aware of our different status, I was called by my surname 'Stead' and the other two were called 'Mister'. I soon learned that anyone wearing a uniform was treated with contempt. I began to settle down to my duties: delivering telegrams to the assistant station masters, station inspectors, parcels department, Wellington Street and Hunslet Lane goods yard. It was all very enjoyable especially as I was provided with a bicycle to ride to the places some distance away.

On night shift the messenger worked the switchboard. This board was one of those where you plugged a wire into the switchboard and then you plugged into the appropriate connection which the caller wished to speak to. My pay for a 48-hour a week was ten shillings (50 pence). The chief clerk, who paid out all the salaries and wages, took great delight in paying me 19 sixpences each week; one sixpence was stopped for my stamp.

In these war years food was very scarce. On one occasion the chief clerk said to me: 'Stand here boy'. (This meant to stand in front of his desk.) He then said: 'You will go to Leeds Market in the 'butchers row' and buy two lbs of horse meat. You will then take it to my house. My wife will take it from you'. He gave me the money plus three pence for my return tram fare. On arrival at his house I gave the lady the horsemeat, saying: 'This is for your dogs', whereupon she looked at me and said 'We don't have a dog!' I could not get back to the station quick enough to tell all and sundry that the chief clerk was eating horsemeat. Of course he soon found out who had let the cat out of the bag so my fate was sealed.

Some of the younger clerks were being called up for war service so the L.M.S. decided to ask some of the retired staff to return to work. Charlie and Arthur returned and fortunately they both tolerated young messengers so I got on well with them both. On one occasion when Charlie and I were on night duty he asked me if I could use a morse key. I told him I could as I had been learning the morse code on the quiet and had become quite proficient. Unfortunately this was to lead to my undoing (more of that later). Cigarettes at the time were very scarce, but I knew every shop in the area and when they were being sold. So now the contemptible messenger in uniform was now called 'Ronnie love, will you try to get me some cigarettes?' I soon became a spiv. Every packet I purchased I made a penny on. In those days two or three shillings was quite a sum. In fact one of the clerks once borrowed two shillings from me. I was now a moneylender! I sometimes ventured into the local pubs such as the Scarboro Taps and the Black Lion to sell cigarettes. Often the ladies of the night who hung out there (by this time lots of American servicemen were based here) would often ask me to sell them cigarettes and often they would borrow a few shillings from me. Mind you, I always got my money back and in cash - not in kind!

One morning Charlie and I were on the early turn. The clerk due on at 7.0am failed to take duty and to make matters worse the clerk due on at 8.0am also failed. Charlie asked me if I would help by sending some telegrams to Derby. Here I must point out that at the time Derby was the HQ of the L.M.S. and everything that happened had to be reported to them. I first called Derby telegraph office and explained the situation; the man said: 'OK get on with it'. I got started with the morse key and was doing nicely when the hairs on the back of my neck started rising as a voice bellowed: 'what the devil are you doing boy, on that morse key?' I tried to explain the situation but he snarled: 'You are a junior porter and not capable of using a morse key'. I said: 'If you ask the man at Derby I think you will find I am'. His parting blow was that I was not to use the morse key again. A couple of weeks later I was sent for and told to stand in front of his desk, I thought this is the end of my railway career. I was quite startled when he said: 'You will become a junior clerk. You will have to go to Pitman's College and learn shorthand and typing. This will, of course be at your own expense'!

On ten bob a week I replied: 'No thank you, I wish to remain a junior porter'. The following Monday I was transferred to a little station between Leeds and Bradford Forster Square. When I arrived there and met the stationmaster, we both knew that we would be the best of enemies.

The stationmaster was a large rotund gentleman, who always wore a bowler hat and had a fearsome reputation. He could reduce grown men to tears with one withering gaze. I had not worked there long when he came to me and said: 'You boy, you will clean the up slow platform waiting room this morning'. I replied: 'Sir, how shall I accomplish that?' 'Go to the stables and bring the hosepipe.' This I did and he then told me to attach the end to this very large tap. All the time he was standing over me with his bowler hat stuck firmly to his head. He said: 'I will turn on the tap and you direct the hosepipe onto the waiting room floor'. The water suddenly gushed out at about 1,000 gallons per minute and I am sure it would have taken at least two experienced firemen to hold onto the hose. I tried to direct it to the waiting room floor but the pipe was like a snake having a fit and had a mind of its own. The result was that the jet blew out all the windows and most of the roof!

In all the confusion I suddenly heard the stationmaster bellowing. Turning round, I discovered the bowler hat rolling about in the deluge and the great man soaked to the skin. It was at this point in time I had the feeling that I probably wasn't his most favourite person. His face was white but as I watched, I could see the colour rising in his throat from pink to red, to purple and slowly creeping into his face. He then raised his fist and came at a run towards me. I let go of the out of control hosepipe and legged it along the platform; fortunately for me youth was on my side. Reaching the end of the platform I turned in blind panic to see that the great man had stopped running but the hosepipe was still doing a merry dance and the whole station area was now flooded. To my relief, he turned the tap off and from some distance away called: 'Come here boy'. I went forward hesitantly and stopped just out of his reach. 'You boy, clean up this mess, I'm going home to change'. He never mentioned the incident again.

When I was the Assistant Station Manager at Leeds I was asked to go and see the Area Manager, who explained that a member of staff was due to be presented with a long service award and as he didn't know the man would I be present to tell him something about him. The ceremony was arranged and I met the recipient and found that he had brought his wife along, who was in a wheelchair. The Manager's office was quite small and it took some time to manoeuvre the chair into the office and when we were all in, the place was quite cramped for room. I had informed the boss all I knew of the

183

man and so he started to ask him questions about his career. Unfortunately, he was one of those chaps who were speechless; he answered every question with just a yes or no. The boss tried to talk to his wife with the same result, so seeking to get it over with the boss took out a large barometer. He then looked at the instrument and tried to explain to the couple how it worked. Now here it became a problem, as being a stranger to Leeds the boss didn't know how high Leeds was above sea level, so he asked me. I immediately replied 132 feet above sea level. He duly set the barometer and handed it over to the man, at the same time complimenting him on his faithful and long service. At this precise moment in the cramped office, the man's wife broke wind to some degree. There was a stunned silence so I opened the door and pushed her out and said goodbye to them both. When I returned to the office the boss was rolling on the floor with laughter. When he had recovered his composure, he said: 'It was fortunate that you knew how many feet Leeds was above sea level'. I said: 'I didn't, it was the first figure that came into my head'. I have since discovered that Leeds is in fact 32 feet above sea level.

THE DELTICS

At 3,300 hp the Deltics set new performance standards on the East Coast main line. The deep-throated engine note screamed power as they hauled the fast express trains along this famous route. Progressively entering service during 1961, they were to be the mainstay of East Coast power for fifteen years, and continued in service until the last one was withdrawn in January 1982. Fortunately, six of these Class 55s have been preserved for posterity. In addition the prototype Deltic is also preserved at the National Railway Museum in York.

Original First Depot number	Second number	Name
D9000 64B*	55022	Royal Scots Grey
D9001 34G	55001	St Paddy
D9002 52A*	55002	The King's Own Yorkshire Light Infantry
D9003 34G	55003	Meld
D9004 64B	55004	Queen's Own Highlander
D9005 Yorkshire	55005 52A	The Prince of Wales's Own Regiment of
D9006 64B	55006	The Fife and Forfar Yeomanry
D9007 34G	55007	Pinza
D9008 52A	55008	The Green Howards

D9009 34G*	55009	Alycidon
D9010 64B	55010	The King's Own Scottish Borderers
D9011 52A	55011	The Royal Northumberland Fusiliers
D9012 34G	55012	Crepello
D9013 64B	55013	The Black Watch
D9014 52A	55014	The Duke of Wellington's Regiment
D9015 34G*	55015	Tulyar
D9016 64B*	55016	Gordon Highlander
D9017 52A	55017	The Durham Light Infantry
D9018 34G	55018	Ballymoss
D9019 64B*	55019	Royal Highland Fusilier
D9020 34G	55020	Nimbus
D9021 64B	55021	Argyll and Sutherland Highlander

* Preserved Locomotives.

Depot Codes.

34G   Finsbury Park, London.
52A   Gateshead.
64B   Haymarket, Edinburgh

CHOLLEY'S STOPPED A HOT ONE

Gordon Reed

In his element - Gordon Reed

Gordon Reed *came from a railway family, his grandfather being a platelayer on the Border Counties Railway of the North British Railway. Two of his uncles were stationmaster and signalling inspector respectively. He even married into a railway family, as his wife was a typist at West Auckland Shed and many of her relatives were connected with the industry. Gordon commenced his career as an apprentice boilersmith at Darlington locomotive works in October 1948. By the time he had completed the five-year apprenticeship he received the call to serve Queen and Country for two years National Service. After basic training he was posted to Marchwood Military Railway to serve with the Royal Engineers. Returning to civilian life in 1956 he was boilersmith examiner at West Auckland motive power depot (Co Durham) until the demise of steam in this area. In 1963 he moved to Dinsdale (Darlington) rail welding depot, before moving to Wellington Street Leeds as track welding inspector for the West Riding. 1974 saw him as Chief Welding Inspector for the Eastern Region and eventually becoming Welding Manager for InterCity E.C.M.L. from which post he retired in 1994.*

I actually came to know Gordon through his son David who continued the family tradition by joining the service in 1982 as a messenger with the Civil Engineers at Leeds. After a time as a fare collector and in the revenue protection team he is currently working as duty shift manager at Arriva Trains Northern Service delivery office York. David inherited that same commitment and enthusiasm to the job that his father had always had. In retirement Gordon keeps busy looking after the steam loco boilers at the Worth Valley Railway and the National Railway Museum. He now recons he is possibly Britain's oldest working boilersmith.

I arrived at Darlington Loco Works as a fresh-faced young boy of 16 years. Working conditions in 1948 were grim but bearable, the hours were 7.30am to 5.00pm, no sick pay for ten years; two years' wait for free travel. The noise was the worst feature, a crescendo of riveting, caulking and heavy platework. Most boilersmiths were deaf by their mid 40s and by retirement many suffered from tinnitus. I recall one occasion when a boilersmith had been killed in an accident. On their arrival Transport Police could not hear anything for the noise and had to interview witnesses in the canteen where they discovered they still had to shout, as all the workers were deaf. In the works if you got hit by a rivet you had 'stopped one'. Most men were hit by cold rivets being punched out of fireboxes etc, but one day a man called Cholley was hit square on the forehead by a hot one. A nasty burn was the result and word went round the shop; Cholley's stopped a hot one. However I really enjoyed my apprenticeship working on many different types of locomotives.

In the repair shop there was a glass tank with small fish in it, they had been in the tender or tanks of locos coming in for general repair and had managed to survive in the couple of inches of water left in the tanks. Starbeck and Whitby engines generally had some marine life in their tanks. The fish arrived via water columns filled by streams and did well to survive the shock. I too was soon to receive a culture shock, commencing my National Service.

After the traditional horrors of military training at Malvern Wells - loads of bullshit, marching, manoeuvres and bromide in tea (to dull our interest in the girls) - I was posted to Southampton. The army railway was based at a military port on the south side of the Solent at a small village called Marchwood where I was to be the unit's boilermaker. The railway serviced a large port complex where vast amounts of fuel, armoured vehicles and the ironwork of what was in 1954 still quite a sizeable British Empire. We had two army 0-6-0 tank engines (J24s), which were painted royal blue with big bold yellow 'M.M.R.' letters on the saddle tanks. The railway operated passenger trains to take soldiers and civvies to and from the docks. Mid morning saw two major events, the daily freight train from B.R. and the arrival of the NAAFI mobile canteen. After the break and some light-hearted banter with the mature but quite curvaceous girl on the NAAFI wagon (no bromide now) the goods train from B.R. would be sorted and shunted into the respective sidings. If ships were under load one loco would be dedicated to this work to shunt as required.

My duties were much like the ones on B.R. except for no heavy repairs. 'Keep them running' was the basic motto. Life continued in this routine with many laughs including an incident when one of our firemen's bath water was laced with a full bottle of Sloan's Liniment (used by sportsmen for aching muscle relief). He got in and leapt out holding his private parts, followed by a prolonged period of cold water on the affected 'fittings'. One day when I was doing a firing turn we approached the port jetty loading area with about ten warflats loaded with tanks, when a road tractor hauling about six trailers cut across in front of us. The loco driver, a full time soldier, sounded the whistle, shut off steam and put the loco into reverse. An impressive slip of volcanic proportions followed nearly sending me on a high-speed visit to the lavatory. However I survived and the tractor and its trailers just made it without impact! Half the fire had gone up the chimney.

In the spring of 1956 as my demob day drew ever nearer a major shock to the system loomed - Suez. Colonel Nasser, the Egyptian dictator, threatened the Suez Canal. Our imperial might in the Middle East was on the line; demob dates meant nothing. The Marchwood Military Railway became suddenly very busy with up to three trains a day from B.R. We had two engines in steam day and night and were excused all parades and guard duties. We loaded our ships for the expeditionary force and they left for the Canal Zone. Ironically the whole expedition turned into a fiasco and humiliation with world opinion forcing a British and French withdrawal. Some ships returned to Marchwood unloaded. I didn't go to Suez and my demob saw me return to the boilershop at Darlington.

In a moment of youthful madness I applied for a boilersmith vacancy at West Auckland (51F for number crunchers). This was the happiest shed in the North of England and where I was to meet my railway sweetheart - no, not a Q6 but my future wife. In the smoky sulphuric atmosphere in which were encompassed mess room, offices, stores, steam raisers' fire, sand drier and ablutions, kind and mostly cheerful drivers, fitters, shedmen, boilersmiths moved in shadowy rituals to service the demands of the steam engine. From the dark confines of this building, engines would emerge to take trains to the crystal clear fresh air heights of Tow Law, Stainmore Summit and Tebay and the smog and smelly areas of industrial Teesside. The messroom was a dark bottle green basic prison cell shared by all. Heating was a black coal fired range and on more than one occasion my mate would place his tin of Co-op baked beans in the oven prior to dinner. About 12.15 the assembled card playing and slumbering gathering would be rudely awakened by an almighty explosion as the unpierced tin finally succumbed to the basic rules of pressure verses strength and pebble dashed the oven sides with baked beans! From the depths of the engine pits I had observed lustfully between the spokes of J27s a delightful apparition, which appeared each morning about 8.30am and disappeared into the office. Fate was on my side when this vision emerged into the shed looking for boilersmith Gordon Reed – the Shedmaster wanted to see me. We met on the turntable and I was in love. Suddenly leaky tubes and stays were not that important. 'Love changes everything' and we married in 1961. Life in the happy shed continued till 1963 when closure came.

After three years with Darlington relayers I arrived at Leeds in the winter of 1966 as the District Track Welding Inspector. It was not an easy start and I had more than my share of problems including a grinding machine hit by a Trans-Pennine diesel express, ripping the train fuel tanks. The area was a district of contrasts from the Barnsley coalfields, the deep valleys of Calderdale to the wonderful scenery of the Harrogate line. My area included the 3rd (Standedge), 4th (Bramhope) and 6th (Morley) longest tunnels on British Rail. We were now in the age of the long welded rail (LWR) and all these tunnels were relayed with the LWR during my time at Leeds. Standedge was a dry inert tunnel with no animal life in it, you never saw a mouse or a moth. Bramhope tunnel was very wet and presented real problems for the welders. As the LWR programme grew I acquired a new generation of welders and won some of the crusty old timers over. Working long, hard Sundays generated big fat pay packets and I was suddenly making big money. One particular Permanent Way Inspector was reputed to earn more than the district engineer!

The Airedale line to Skipton was a main line to us but to the London Midland Region a branch line. I recall one Saturday night at Kildwick level crossing; the permanent way supervisor had obviously struggled with his maths as he shouted to his gang: 'Half of you go that way taking off fish plates, half of you go over the crossing and knock out clips and the rest of you come with me'! Good old Joe. On occasions we would have a Sunday possession on the Settle and Carlisle line and Joe's famous clarion call shouted at about 3.00pm to all and sundry was 'The Scotch has left Appleby'. This was the Glasgow-London express and meant there was about an hour left before handing back the line for trains. My section became a key element of the track modernisation programme and grew to about 24 men. In 1975 there was a vacancy for the Eastern Region Chief Welding Inspector based at York. I was successful in my application and now covered an area from King's Cross to Berwick, Felixstowe to Filey! Quality was the key and my job was to reduce the number of broken welds and rails, a major cause of train delays. Funny incidents (luckily without injury) included a relaying job at Aycliffe on the East Coast Main Line when a ballast train became divided and one section passed the welders on the other line without a loco and five minutes later returned to repeat the run one more time. The chargehand welder, Walter Blower, muttered: 'There's something funny going on'.

ANGLO SCOTS

31st July 1873: North British Railway introduced first sleeping cars between Glasgow Queen Street and London King's Cross and vice versa.

1st July 1876: Pullman Cars introduced between Glasgow St Enoch and St Pancras, Drawing room cars on day service and sleeping cars on night trains.

13th August 1888: Race to Edinburgh. 10.00am Euston to Edinburgh Princes Street in 426 minutes.

31st August 1888: 10.00am King's Cross to Edinburgh Waverley in 408 minutes.

3rd July 1893: Dining cars introduced between London St Pancras and Glasgow St Enoch.

21st August 1895: Race to Aberdeen. 8.00pm King's Cross to Aberdeen arrived 4.40am.

22nd August 1895: 8.00pm Euston to Aberdeen arrived 4.32am.

1st August 1890: Dining cars introduced on 10.00am King's Cross to Edinburgh and vice versa. The 20-minute luncheon stop at York abolished.

1st May 1928: LNER. Flying Scotsman non-stop between Edinburgh and King's Cross.

5th July 1937: LMS. Coronation Scot introduced six and half-hour journey between Glasgow and London.

5th July 1937: LNER. Coronation introduced six hour journey between Edinburgh and London.

15th June 1955: First car carrying train ran King's Cross to Perth and vice versa.

17th March 1979: Penmanshiel Tunnel (near Grantshouse) collapsed whilst being enlarged. Two contractors' men killed. Line diverted around tunnel and reopened 20th August 1979.

ROMANCE AT THE DOUBLE

Peter Brooks

Who's a lucky boy then?
Peter Brooks doing a hard days work!

Liverpool born **Peter Brooks** *commenced his career with the railway on the 28th April 1950 as a junior porter. He passed to be a train recorder working in Walton Junction signal box and progressed to working in many of the local Liverpool cabins. In September 1952 he was called for National Service, serving with the Royal Air Force.*

On returning to the railway a much wiser man he decided to stay in the signalling grade and his first post was at Fazakerley Station signal box. Peter progressed through the signalling grades until by 1961 he had attained the position of special class relief signalman. In 1965 he moved into the supervisory ranks by becoming station inspector at Accrington. In 1967 he moved to London Marylebone station as an operating inspector. After a spell back at Liverpool he became signal box supervisor at Newport High Street and Old Oak Common. He entered the managerial grade as assistant station manager at Leeds Station, after a short period spent in a temporary capacity at Slough. Peter retired in 1998 having given 48 years of dedicated service

*and is now able to devote more time to his hobbies of model
railways, model trams and road transport. He also gives much
of his time as secretary to The Leeds Branch British Rail Retired
Staff Association.*

I was born and raised in the Fazakerly and Aintree Districts of
Liverpool, approximately seven miles from the City Centre. I was
six years of age when the Second World War commenced in
September 1939. At the time my two sisters and I were living with
our grandparents. As we were growing up I was always playing
with Dinky Toy motors, lorries, trams and buses, which was to develop
into a lifetime's interest. Meccano at Binns Road, Liverpool, produced
these toys. Hornby was also renowned for its products and are still
much sought after to this day. On one side of my grandparent's
house was a very large playing field, which belonged to Queen Mary's
High School. As small children we used to watch the girls playing
various sports as our garden fence bordered the school grounds.
Sadly, the outbreak of war saw the fields commandeered for the
building of a Royal Ordnance Factory, which was to produce arms
and ammunition for the war effort. Our house stood in the grounds
of Nelsons Preserving Company, a jam factory in other words. They
turned out jams, jellies, and preserved fruits for the armed forces.
Throughout the war my grandmother used to provide meals for the
Auxiliary Fire Service Station at the nearby Jacobs Biscuit works.
One Christmas I was given the most beautiful cart and trailer I had
ever seen, my grandmother would load the food on to it and I would
deliver it to the fire station so I suppose this was my earliest contact
with transport.

As the war waged on we had some near misses, as the German
bombers were not very accurate. Prime targets such as the Cheshire
Lines Railway, the Royal Ordnance Works and factories like Nelson's,
Jacob's and Hartley's who were supplying the forces with
ammunition, arms and food, were rarely hit but the cemetery across
the road received one hell of an hammering. However, none of the
occupants ever complained! Mounds of earth and sand were built

up as protection in front of the factories but one night the raiders dropped three high explosive bombs into one of these mounds which failed to explode and they were to remain there until well after the war was over when they were made safe and eventually removed. We were confined to an air raid shelter at the rear of the factory for three days until it was thought safe for us to come out. Supplies, including arms and ordnance were transported via nearby sidings to the factories and one such train of ammunition was bombed (fortunately for us, further down the line) causing quite an explosion.

The day came in December 1948 when, at 15 years of age, I was let loose on an unsuspecting big bad world. I found that I now had to work for a living and became an office boy in a Liverpool solicitors' office, being paid the princely sum of twenty seven shillings per week (£1.35.) I then moved on to become an apprentice chef at the Stork Hotel, Liverpool, but still had not found my niche and became a shop boy at a local greengrocer's. By now thoroughly fed up with myself at not having found a career I felt I could be happy in I decided to try the railway. I applied to the local stationmaster and after an interview and medical I commenced my railway career as a train recorder at Liverpool Walton Junction signal box. My pay was forty four shillings (£2.20) per week, quite an increase to what I had been earning since leaving school. This was the start of a career that was to last for forty-eight years and six months. After a while I progressed to relief signal box lad, which included covering for junior porters, junior ticket collectors and junior telegraph messengers in the Liverpool Exchange, Southport and Ormskirk areas. September 1952 saw me arrive at R.A.F. Padgate (Warrington) for two years' National Service. I then moved to Innsworth, Gloucester for basic training and on to the School of Cookery. After a short period we were drafted to Canvey Island, Essex to set up kitchens to feed the troops. They were being drafted in to sandbag the area against the massive floods that had occurred during the night, killing a number of people and flooding the area. After the emergency was over I returned to Gloucester and successfully passed my exams after which I served out the rest of my time at Netheravon, on Salisbury Plain.

Returning to the railway I commenced training at the Manchester Victoria School of Signalling. While there I became friendly with a young lady who worked in the telephone exchange located in the same building. We were getting along fine when some of my colleagues guessed what was happening and scrawled in the dust on the corridor windows 'Peter loves Margaret'. When the resident instructor saw it he demanded to know who it was who was seeing his niece, oops! Undaunted, I continued to see her but then started seeing another young lady who worked in the buffet where we had our tea breaks. Unfortunately, it wasn't long before they got their heads together and realised that they were both going out with the same guy. Oops! again. Double romance came to an abrupt end.

After reaching the top of the signalling grades I thought I would try to gain promotion to supervisory status. This was to prove difficult as the local stationmaster had taken a distinct disliking to me as he thought I was trying to get above my station in life. Eventually a replacement stationmaster came on the scene who gave me every encouragement to get on. Returning home from Walton Junction signal box at 10.00pm one night I alighted from the bus near my local railway station to find there had been an incident on the rail track. A report had been received that a train near the station had hit someone. I took charge of the events being the first railway employee on the scene. I discovered the body of a woman just past the station so opened up the local signal box and immediately stopped all trains in the vicinity. I alerted the emergency services and the stationmaster and it was 3.00am the following morning before I returned home. The stationmaster at Liverpool Exchange recommended me for an award and commendation which I duly received and my career took off from there as I was appointed station inspector at Accrington Station.

The next few years saw me move to various locations in London and the immediate area then to South Wales. In 1981 I was appointed to Assistant Station Manager at Leeds from which position I retired in 1998. In the course of my sojourn in to the London Area I had the good fortune to meet a young lady from Liverpool (my home city). By a mischance, we were staying in the same lodgings but this time I was not two-timing. Romance blossomed to the extent we were married in September 1974. After 17 years of very happy marriage and at the end of four years of suffering from cancer that same young lady passed away.

I can honestly say that I have enjoyed my career on the railways, made many friends and no doubt some enemies along the way but I have no regrets of my decision all those years ago to join that great institution…'The Railway' – railwaymen were and still are a breed of their own showing great devotion to duty through thick and thin.

During my period on British Railways I came into contact with the travelling public on a regular basis. I repeat here a letter sent in by one such member:

Dear British Rail
I have regularly used trains over the last eleven years and although the service is not always first class this is the first time I have taken pen to paper to comment though this is a complaint with a difference and I'm still laughing about it. Tonight I travelled on the 5.14pm from Bradford, which was due to stop at my home station of Church Fenton. When the train stopped at Leeds, unbeknown to others and me it was divided into two portions. The front portion departed for Church Fenton leaving our portion stranded in the Leeds platform. We alighted from the train that was going nowhere to complain to station staff. We were informed we would have to wait another hour, so I decided to complain to a higher level, your Assistant Station Manager. He kindly arranged to stop the next Newcastle express at Church Fenton especially just for me. I was delighted. However, I just thought you might like to know you had the last laugh, although as I said before, I too had a good laugh. As the train slowed down to stop at Church Fenton I pulled down the window to open the door. The inertia caused by the braking brought a cascade

of water, icy cold I might add, down on my head, coat and feet. I alighted from the train in fits of laughter and laughed all the way home. Thank you for brightening my day.

Yours drippingly.

Letter from a passenger who had lost his filofax and had not noticed:

Thank you very much indeed for forwarding my lost property on to me, especially with such speed and after so much confusion as to which of us many brothers it should go to. It might have been a disaster if my brothers had got their hands on my rather minute list of numbers of my girlfriends! Thank you again for your help, please find enclosed £5 for postal charges.

MORE OF COVA

Rumours: 'Never believe a rumour until it is officially denied'. Statement by a French official at a meeting attended with French National Railways (SNCF).

An American railroad official complained that getting anything decided was equal to mating elephants. It was done at a very high level, it was accompanied by a tremendous amount of noise and it took 18 months to get results.

Eurostar drivers who operate trains between London, Paris and Brussels are trained to speak French and English so they can converse with controllers and other railway staff on both sides of the Channel Tunnel. An English driver, speeding across northern France one day spotted a large stag near the line side. Not knowing the French word for stag, he told the French control office, in his limited French, that what he had seen was 'a cow with a pantograph'.

The class 9E electric locomotives of South Africa are 50 KV AC machines used on heavy ore haulage. The trains they haul are so long that each locomotive is equipped with a motorcycle, carried in a case under the frame. If the driver needs to attend to a defect along the train, he jumps on his motorbike to ride to the wagon giving trouble.

For trainmen working on the Ginza subway line in Tokyo, a special amenity is provided at the end of the platform at the terminus of Shibuya. This comprises a small refrigerator. Here the conductor will pick up a cool drink and a cold towel for the driver and himself. A most welcome relief on a hot summer's day.

For many years, drivers of diesel and electric trains have been at risk from bird strikes when working at high speeds where a bird hitting the front of the train could penetrate the windscreen

201

of the driving cab. In an effort to provide a better degree of safety (and to reduce delays) research was done to find a suitable toughened glass windscreen for drivers. As part of this research, advice was sought from airline windscreen suppliers, who suggested a good test for any new glass type was to fire a chicken at high speed towards the window material. The test was duly set up and a number of dead chickens obtained.

The test with the first chicken showed that the glass was not tough enough, even though it was of a standard used by the airlines. A second test also smashed the glass. Another test smashed the third windscreen. Repeated attempts showed that no glass could stand up to the chicken being fired at it. More advice was sought from the airline people, who could not understand why the glass they offered could withstand airborne bird strikes but persistently failed the railway test.

They decided to come and witness the tests. The railway research team set up a new test and sent someone to obtain more chickens. When the chickens arrived, it was then the airline experts realised what was wrong. They told the railway research team: 'You know, you have to defrost the chickens first'!

WOR ABART THAT WOODBINE THA OWES MI?

Peter Kirton

Author Peter Kirton - enjoying retirement

*I have known **Peter Kirton** for almost 69 years – longer than anyone else in this book. Born in Normanton, he came from a family for whom the coal mines had been the major employment. Peter didn't want to do that, so he joined the railway as a book lad at Goose Hill Junction signal box. At 18 he was called up for National Service, for part of which he served in Kenya. On his return he became a signalman, initially at a succession of cabins but later on relief. Seeing that the signalman was a dying breed he moved to York and into carriage cleaning but that didn't last long, as his job was done away with.*

Ticket inspecting was his next metier and he became a Travelling Ticket Inspector at Leeds, where he rose until he was the Chief Ticket Inspector there. His last move was in a similar role, that of a Senior Trains Inspector for InterCity, responsible for training and supervising the InterCity Senior Conductors. Finally he reached the dizzy height of Route Chief Trains Inspector for InterCity East Coast, which led him to meet a lot of eminent

203

people. Peter retired in 1993 and since then he has been bitten by the writing bug, with two books to his name (so far). How appropriate that one who started as a book lad should finish as one! He also likes listening to people talking about their railway careers and persuading them to repeat their stories in front of a microphone. Having asked, requested, cajoled, solicited, pleaded, implored, persuaded, invited, begged and even bribed for the price of a pint of beer, the many railwaymen for the numerous personal stories in this book; he felt it only fair that he too should make a contribution. This has led to his next book – this one. Who knows? – maybe there is more to follow!

My railway career began as a young train recorder in Goose Hill Junction Signal Box at Normanton. In 1836 three Acts of Parliament were passed for three railways that would converge on Normanton. The North Midland Railway from Derby to Leeds reached Normanton in June 1840 and was opened throughout on 1st July 1840. This was to become the Midland Railway (10th May 1844). The Manchester to Leeds trans-Pennine railway came down the Calder Valley to meet the Derby to Leeds line at Goose Hill Junction and reached Normanton on the 5th October 1840 and would eventually become the Lancashire & Yorkshire Railway (9th July 1847). George Hudson's York & North Midland Railway joined the North Midland at Altofts Junction on the 1st July 1840 and became the North Eastern Railway (31st July 1844). Normanton Joint Station was opened in 1841 followed by a hotel, which allowed clients to walk via the arched canopy station entrance without being exposed to the elements. The railways brought to life what had been a small agricultural village and transformed it into a thriving coal mining and industrial town.

The Manchester-Leeds timetable for 1844 reflects the importance of Normanton Station and its hotel. A rider to the timetable states: 'Very superior accommodation is afforded at the Normanton Hotel for those passengers or families wishing to go to London, York, Hull, Newcastle etc, by the earliest trains'. 'Passengers can travel on the two latest trains from Manchester, stay overnight at the hotel and travel to their destinations the following morning'. In addition to first and second class carriages, many of these trains conveyed 'Stanhopes', which were 17 feet long open trucks with no seats. This was to afford the poorer classes the convenience of third class travel. However, the Company's servants were strictly forbidden to porter for such wagon passengers.

In 1870 the station was re-modelled and with platforms nearly a quarter mile long (the fourth longest in the country) it was known as the 'Crewe of the North'. In 1876 The Midland Railway opened its through route to Scotland via Leeds and Carlisle and as restaurant cars had not been invented, Normanton was designated the 30 minute refreshment stop for these services both north and south. The first class passengers taking their meals in the hotel, and third class passengers in the large station refreshment rooms. Many famous people were to stop off at Normanton for a meal, including Queen Victoria, Prime Ministers Gladstone and Disraeli, President of USA, Ulysses S Grant and Emperor of Brazil Dom Pedro II. In 1894 restaurant cars were introduced so the station lost some of its importance but even by 1928 it employed 900 staff, had a busy engine shed and several marshalling yards, sorting 18,000 wagons each week and over 400 trains passing through in a 24 hour period.

My railway career began as a train recorder in Goose Hill Junction Signal Box on the 13th March 1951. Escorted to the cabin by a station porter I climbed about a dozen steps and walked into a strange and totally bewildering new world. The first thing that struck me was the pungent smell of the place, a mixture of tobacco, paraffin, coal burning stove, floor polish, black lead and Brasso. The signal box was quite long for it contained 64 levers of various colours, above which was the block instrument shelf that also contained various shaped bells for sending and receiving coded signals. Another signalman has described the function of the levers, block instruments and bells elsewhere in this book, so I will not repeat the process. Goose Hill was open every day of the year, 24 hours a day and was worked by a signalman and train recorder on a three shift system: 6.00am to

2.00pm, 2.00pm to 10.00pm and 10.00pm to 6.00am. It was my job to decipher all the bells signals sent and received by the signalman and enter them in the train register. On average there were seven bell signals and therefore seven entries in the train register for every train that passed the signal box and these had to be entered at the precise minute. In addition I had to telephone a report to the control office of all train movements every 15 minutes.

The train recorder who worked the early turn from 6.00am to 2.00pm was responsible for carrying out all the domestic duties. The daily routine was to ensure that the water supply was replenished, to fill and carry enough buckets of coal into the cabin to last for the three shifts, to trim and fill the paraffin hand lamp ready for the night shift, to empty the accumulated ashes from the coal stoves; sweep the floor and dust the telephones, block instruments and other indicators. The weekly routine was to clean all the windows, a very daunting task which sometimes took hours of arm-aching work out on a shaky verandah, often in bitterly cold weather. The cabin floor had to be washed with water collected from a large drum outside, which was connected to the gutters. The coal stoves had to be black-leaded, a messy job that made a person look like they had done a shift down the local coalmine. All the instrument brasses and the signal levers had to be cleaned and polished. While these tasks were being performed the signalman would endeavour to carry out the train recorder's duties so it was very rare that the early turn team could sit back and relax.

Pulling signal levers could at times be a very dangerous occupation. Every lever in every signal box had its own characteristics and signalmen had to know just how much pressure was required, whether pulling a lever off or reversing it back into the frame. If the signal wire broke while he was having a real good pull at one of these levers, the signalman could shoot into the back of the cabin and quite often sustain a serious injury. Point levers were generally the heaviest to pull. They had to be pulled to move the points one way and then pushed to move them back again. Because of this pull-push action the connection between the points and the signal box was made of metal rodding. Sets of points that were some distance from the cabin were always a problem, especially if the lever changed both sets of points at a crossover. To maintain the points in good working order and for ease of movement, they were cleaned and oiled every day by the platelayers.

Having completed my three weeks of training I commenced my duties as a train recorder. In the process I had been subjected to the usual signalman's pranks that all the book lads fell for such as: being told in a serious voice to keep pulling and reversing a certain white lever in order to wind the clock up on the wall; being sent to the chief clerks office to collect the 'monthly edition of the weekly fortnight'; asking the driver of a stationary engine for a bucket of steam; being sent to the lamp-man's cabin to ask for some red paraffin for the stop signals and some green paraffin for the proceed signals. I would in time play the same pranks on new unsuspecting boys. I learned a lesson in cooking very early in my railway career, having taken a tin of beans for my breakfast on the early turn. My signalman said, 'Just put the tin in a pan of water and put it on top of the stove to heat up', he failed to mention that I should first put two holes in the tin and at the time I knew no better. Having got very busy with trains, I completely forgot about the beans until suddenly there was a terrific explosion and my beans had pebble-dashed the signal box roof. Some weeks later the painters came and did not bother to remove my beans but simply painted over them. They tell me when the box was taken down my beans was still in situ and everyone thought they were knots in the wood!

The railway at this period was a very busy and dangerous place. Today there are very strict rules about walking on or near the track and everyone who does so has had to attend a track safety course and pass an examination. In the fifties, no one received any training and as a result many lives were lost over the years simply because many people did not know the basics of track safety. I had only been working at Goose Hill a couple of months when it was brought home to me what a dangerous place the rail track was. One morning, two men walked past our box on their way to a place about a quarter of mile towards St John's. They were both carrying picks and shovels and my signalman shouted to them as they past that they would make good gravediggers. About ten minutes later the down express from St Pancras to Leeds approached us braking heavily. The driver ran back to us and shouted he had just hit two men who had stepped in front of a stationary train directly into the path of the express. Both men who had just walked by our box had been killed instantly.

One day I was working at Altofts Junction Signal Box as a train recorder on the 6.00am to 2.00pm shift. I was working with a signalman who was regarded as a very blunt Yorkshire man. Jackie Jones the Normanton stationmaster had sent a note saying he would be visiting the signal cabin along with some very senior managers from York. Mr Jones was a pipe smoker but he also had a reputation for helping himself to the signalman's cigarettes if they had been left out on the desk. When he was on his rounds the signalmen would warn each other: 'Look out Jackie's on his way, put your fags out of sight'. On the morning of the visit by the York people, Jackie and they first inspected the track and the junction outside of the cabin and after about 20 minutes they came inside. Jackie a small plump gentleman pulled himself up to his full height and said, putting on his best official voice to make a good impression on the York officials: 'Good morning signalman, I trust everything is in order?' My signalman's reaction was: 'What's up wi thee, Jackie?' 'As tha forgotton mi name?' The stationmaster was clearly embarrassed and said: 'Carry on with your duties signalman'. My signalman did just that, taking no notice of Mr Jones or the VIPs. As the party stood at the door ready to depart, the stationmaster thought he would recover some of his dignity: 'Thank you signalman, keep up the good work'. 'Just a minute Jackie' came the reply, 'As tha forgotten summat?' 'Wor abart that Woodbine tha owes mi?'

On reaching the age of 18, like most young men of the time I was called up for my two years National Service, joining the King's Own

Yorkshire Light Infantry. I was to serve my time in Berlin and Kenya and, although there were plenty of rough times, in the main I enjoyed it so much I stayed in the Territorial Army for a further ten years. Returning to civilian life I passed out to be a signalman, my first box just dealing with goods traffic. Progressing to main line signalling, I then moved to spells on the former Great Northern Railway at Balne Lane, Wakefield and Whithams on the old Lancashire & Yorkshire Railway, before returning to Normanton Station North as a class I signalman. Now being a married man and needing the money, I managed to become a general purpose relief signalman working at any one of 15 different signal cabins.

One of the loneliest signal boxes I worked at was called Waterloo, which was situated on the Leeds side of Woodlesford Station. Because of its isolation it was never a popular box to work in and vacancies cropped up quite often. Some cabins had a cosy atmosphere and appearance – not so Waterloo. The main function of the box was controlling the coal traffic into Skelton Grange Power Station. It was ironic that we were supplying the power station with the fuel to enable it to pump millions of watts of electricity into the power supply and yet the only lighting we had was a paraffin Tilley lamp hung over the train register. The only means of boiling water was by the coal stove, the water being delivered by a light engine each day. The toilet was a dry one and only used in an extreme emergency. Due to its location it was not the place to work for anyone of a nervous disposition.

At one period there were two vacancies at the cabin. Another Normanton man called Frank and I were covering them. The third signalman at Waterloo was called Bill and he had worked there for about twenty years. It so happened that Frank and Bill were bitter enemies and after we had been working there for some weeks, Bill said to me when I was relieving him: 'Does your feet get black when you have been working in here for eight hours?' I replied: 'No, not really'. He said: 'Well mine do, look I'll show you'. Bill took off his shoes and socks and sure enough his feet were really black.

Like many signallers Bill had an old pair of shoes he kept in the cabin all the time. He put on his socks and walking out shoes and put his work shoes up on the shelf ready for when he came on duty next day. Eight hours later when Frank came to relieve me I mentioned to him about Bill's feet getting black. 'Yes' he said: 'They will do, before he comes on duty I put a spoonful of soot in his shoe toe from the back of the coal stove. Don't tell him!' A few days later Frank complained to me: 'Do you know Pete, I had the runs terrible yesterday, I must have gone to the toilet 15 times in eight hours'. When I next relieved Bill I told him about Frank having the runs bad. 'That will teach him a lesson' Bill said, 'I know he's been pinching my sugar out of my locker so I emptied half of it out of the jar and topped it up with Epsom salts, he won't pinch my sugar again'.

The signal box at Woodlesford Station was situated on the platform and in stark contrast to Waterloo, was considered quite cosy. It had the benefit of gas lighting and was in pleasant surroundings even though it still only had a dry toilet and the water had to be brought by a porter each day from the station buildings. Directly across from the cabin was the stationmaster's house. Each day the stationmaster, Tom Swaby, would visit the box to sign the train register as required by the rules. Mr Swaby was one of the old-time railwaymen and a real gentleman. We also used to get another visitor from the Swaby household in the shape of his cat, which would cross the lines and jump up on to the platform and come into the box for any titbits we may have. I used to say to Tom: 'You know Mr Swaby, that cat of yours will be getting run over crossing all those lines every day'. 'Peter', he said in a dead serious voice, 'it knows the timetable backwards; it knows when every train is due'. A few weeks later poor Tom's cat lost the last of its nine lives. The next time he came in the box I said: 'I told you Mr Swaby; your cat would get run over'. He again replied in a dead serious voice: 'Yes Peter it did, but it was a special train that the cat didn't know about.

On the 29th April 1967 the new Power Signal Box at Leeds was due to open. This new signalling centre would take the place of all the old signal boxes in the vicinity of Leeds. At the time there were rumours that the area covered by the power box would spread considerably. I thought the situation out carefully and considered it was maybe time to look for another job outside of the signal box. I applied and had interviews for supervisory jobs at Newcastle and Sheffield but without success; my third attempt was for the position of Carriage Cleaning Supervisor at Clifton Carriage Sidings, York. This time I had a successful interview and was informed I had been appointed to the job with a transfer date to York of Monday 29th July 1968. It was going to be a big wrench leaving the signalling grade but I had made the decision so it was now up to me to make a success of it. The signal box had been my home throughout all my working life. All this was about to change and there would be no going back to the signalling grade if I didn't like my new job. I was leaving colleagues and workmates with whom I had associated for the last 17 years; on my arrival at York every person whom I would meet would be a complete stranger. Although we only lived 25 miles away, I would be working all three shifts and some weekends so I would have to fined lodging accommodation for myself. Later still would be the problem of selling our home and buying one in York for my wife and two small children.

There were approximately 30 cleaners for the three shifts and a supervisor for each. The whole depot was worked on a bonus scheme and every cleaning task had been awarded a certain unit value. The maximum number of units a cleaner could earn in an eight-hour shift was 40. If for example I had eight staff on duty I would multiply this by 40, making a maximum total of 320 units. At the end of the shift I would total up all the jobs performed in unit values aiming to arrive at somewhere near the 320 mark. The two other shifts would do likewise and the depot would be awarded a collective bonus for the previous 24 hours. This job opened up a whole new dimension of the railway that I had never appreciated before. Besides the cleaning staff there was a joiner who carried out minor repairs to the coaches, an electrician for the lighting and power, a plumber who serviced the water supply and toilets as well as the restaurant cars. Fitters from the Carriage & Wagon (C&W) department maintained the running gear of the coaches and even a blacksmith appeared periodically to carry out routine servicing. I was amazed at the amount of work that went on behind the scenes, of which I was now a major part!

Something that I found difficult to come to terms with was my newfound freedom to be able to wander about the wash sheds and yards. Until now all my working life had been in a signal box, where even a simple matter like nipping out to the toilet had to be carefully timed and the signalmen on each side informed. The first few months were an extensive learning cycle; I made my share of mistakes but usually only the once. On the night shift Ada came to me and said; 'Pete, the anti-macassars on the London train need changing'. I had no idea what she was talking about but bluffed my way with the reply: 'Yes, will you do the necessary?' She went to the first class section and removed the seat headrest covers and replaced them with clean ones. So, that's what anti-macassars are, another lesson learned.

Another lesson I soon learned nearly cost me my life: I had sent my team into the wash shed to commence cleaning the main line sets while I proceeded into the sidings to obtain the numbers of other trains to be cleaned. It was a clear warm night – perfect weather in fact and I was writing down coach numbers while stupidly standing in the four-foot between the rails. There was not a sound to be heard but for some reason I looked towards the station and there, bearing down on me just three yards away was a parcels van. I flung myself to one side as it brushed by me. I had forgotten the golden rule 'Never look out with your ears'!

Another character in my team was called George. I was never sure if he was an Irishman or a Scotsman as at times is allegiance varied. George would spend his break time making out betting slips, but ask him to take down some coach numbers and it was beyond his capability. He always knew how much the bookmaker owed him, but each week he would ask me to calculate his earnings. One day he requested a lieu-day for the following

Wednesday. I said: 'George put it in writing as the staff office have to keep a record'. Next day he handed me a single sheet of toilet paper, on it was written in pencil: 'Loo day, George'. Another lesson learned! A major part of our work was the York to Inverness Car Sleeper train, which departed several times a week. I always regarded this train as an 88-bed hotel on wheels, as we had to attain the same high standards that would be required in a high-class hotel. During winter, unless the coaches had been connected to the steam heating pipes it was like working in a fridge for the women making the beds. In the summer it could be just the opposite and like working in a greenhouse. On one hot summer day one of the younger women resorted to making the beds just dressed in a bikini. As soon as word got round it was amazing how many joiners, plumbers and C&W staff realised they had a job to do in one of the bedrooms. I soon had to enforce a dress code to stop temperatures rising even higher.

I had been at my job at Clifton Carriage Sidings for nearly three years to the day when I received a letter informing me I had been made redundant. It did not exactly come out of the blue but it was still a shock. The shed was to be reduced from three shifts to two and as I was the last supervisor in, I was the first out. I had never been over the moon with my job at Clifton, seeing it more as a means of getting on the supervisory ladder, but the time spent there had been invaluable. I now had a good knowledge of all types of rolling stock, train and yard working, maintenance of vehicles and supervision of staff, which would come in very handy for the rest of my career. The only problem was that at this moment in time I did not have a career, so it was a matter of scanning the vacancy lists with some urgency. My luck changed when after an interview at Leeds I was appointed to the post of travelling ticket inspector, based at Leeds Divisional Manager's Office (DMO).

This opened up yet another new side of the railway and it was to be one that I really enjoyed. I was given a letter of authority to take to Burton's, the tailors, to be measured for my new uniform. This was a very smart dark grey, three-piece lounge suit. I was also measured for a dark blue Crombie-style overcoat. I also received white shirts and plain grey ties. To complete my kit I was issued with a hat in the style of a French policeman's kepi, with a gold laurel leaf round the band. The hat and its BR double arrow logo was the only evidence I worked for the railway. The reason for that was that sometimes we would be required to go under cover to detect someone travelling fraudulently. The chief ticket inspector at the time was called Wilf and he told me he would supervise my training. I quickly had to become very conversant with all types of tickets and the conditions attached including excess regulations. A good knowledge of the working timetable and passenger working was essential and I spent hours studying the Railway Byelaws, which formed an integral part of the job.

Wilf was a good old railwayman who could tell some wonderful tales. We were once travelling together on a train from Leeds to York. The train stopped at Ulleskelf and a crowd of passengers boarded all without tickets. As this was an unmanned station I commenced selling tickets to these passengers from my excess book while Wilf puffed away on his pipe in the guard's van. Realising I would have a job to sell everyone a ticket before arriving in York, I returned to Wilf and asked him to give me a hand. He looked at me sheepishly and then said: 'I can't'. 'Why not,' I replied. He said: 'I can't spell Ulleskelf'! I never knew if he was pulling my leg or not, but I finished up selling all the tickets. One day I was waiting for a train on platform 5 at Leeds Station when a Manchester to York train pulled in. A smart gentleman walked up to me and said: 'Is this the York train?' 'Yes sir it is'. 'Then why does it say Hull on the window labels?' I could not resist a flippant reply: 'it says 'Heinz Beans' on the side of busses, but they don't sell them! 'The man's face went livid with rage. 'Do you know who I am?' he said. 'No' I replied, 'but I have the feeling you are going to tell me. 'I am the new Chief Operating Superintendent and I am not impressed with you'. I thought: 'Well Pete, if your going to drop a clanger make sure it's a big one.

There was an amusing incident at York Station one morning in the early 1980s. The train announcers worked in the power signal box. Whenever there was an alteration to the script the signal box supervisor would scribble a note and pass it back to the announcer. The announcer would then convert the message into a language the public could understand. The young announcer was comparatively new to the job. On this occasion the poor girl just read out the message as it had been handed to her. It came out something like this to a very surprised public: 'Ladies and Gentlemen, the next train to arrive in platform 8 will be the 0840 to London King's Cross, calling at Doncaster, Grantham, Peterborough and due to arrive at King's Cross at 1113 Will passengers please note that today the restaurant car will be at the arse-end of the train? Oh dear, I'm sorry. I should have said at the rear of the train'.

One Sunday afternoon while waiting for the London train at York exit ticket barriers at train arrived from the north. Among the passengers who alighted was a Newcastle ticket inspector called Barney. He was escorting towards the exit a man who was rather unsteady on his feet. By the time Barney and the man had reached the barrier everyone else had passed through. The man looked very much the worse for drink and in a mean mood. Barney shouted to me: 'Don't let him out – he hasn't paid the fare from Newcastle yet. I'll go and get the police'. He was Barney's prisoner and the rules were that he, Barney, should have detained him while I alerted the police. Barney disappeared whereupon the man decided that he wasn't staying around to meet the police or pay his fare. He started to walk out of the exit barrier but I was in his way, so he tried to push me to one side. In order to stop him I had to push him back. Unfortunately, he fell on his back; the look on his face and the choice words he called me left me in no doubt as to what he would do when he got to his feet. I immediately dropped on top of him to restrain him until the police arrived. The man had other ideas and was determined to get to his feet in order to kick hell out of me. A desperate struggle ensued. As I was trying to pin both his arms to the ground, I felt a tap on my shoulder: Glancing up, I saw a woman and two small children standing over me: 'What time does the Blackpool train go?' She enquired. Still trying to prevent the man from choking me, I croaked 'twenty past three', and then turned my attention to the ensuing struggle. A few seconds later there was another tapping on my shoulder. I again looked up. 'What platform does it go from?' I released his hand from my neck and just managed to say 'platform 14'. She then said: 'It's a pity you have nothing better to do on a Sunday afternoon than act the fool'!

I was to spend a total of 17 enjoyable years as a ticket inspector, the last five of which I was the chief in charge of a team of ten based at Leeds and three inspectors based at Sheffield. In January 1988 I joined the team forming the new grade of trains inspectors becoming the Senior Trains Inspector, Leeds. Our duties combined both operating and commercial, so it opened up another new side of the railway too me. On a test train from King's Cross to Leeds during the summer of 1989, trains inspector Graham Briggs and I were making ourselves conversant with the miniature circuit breakers of the new mark IV coaches, which are situated in a secure compartment at the end of each coach. (Circuit breakers are to all intents and purposes, fuses.) At the time the train was travelling at about 125 miles per hour. We had carried out tests that involved isolating the interior coach sliding doors into the permanent open position. One of us tripped a wrong circuit breaker and the train started to come to a halt very quickly. This was unfortunate for the steward who had just left the restaurant car, balancing a tray of cups of tea intended for the technicians working in the front cab. The train pulled up so fast that the poor man shot past us like a rocket and went his length in the centre aisle, with the cups flying through the air about six feet in front of him. The air was blue with his language. We could hear the conversation between the front and rear cab technicians coming over the public address system. There was a heated conversation between them each blaming the other for the sudden stop. We hastily returned the circuit breaker to its original position, closed and locked the panel door and went to assist the steward. The poor man was fuming. He picked up the remnants

216

of the cups saying: 'If that's how they drive this bloody train, in future they can bring their own tea'. I said: 'I don't blame you mate, they could have told you they were going to do an emergency stop'. Graham and I maintained a low profile for the rest of the journey.

On a journey from King's Cross to Edinburgh a con man took a seat in the restaurant car and ordered lunch plus a bottle of expensive wine, after examining the whole range on offer. Throughout the meal he complimented the two waiters on the excellent service they were giving him. 'He said to them: 'Have yourselves a couple of whiskies each and put them on my bill'. When I entered the restaurant car to check passengers' tickets the man shouted before I even reached him: 'What would you like to drink young man?' My reply was: 'Could I see your ticket please?' 'Ticket, I don't need a ticket'. 'I am related to the Queen. How dare you ask me for a ticket?' Following further questions, I said to the chief steward 'He's a tramp of no fixed abode'. The chief steward said: 'I thought he was a con-man', He's done me for nearly 40 quid. On arrival at Peterborough we alighted and I introduced him to a BT police officer. He told the officer that he was related to the Duke of Gloucester. The officer was suitably impressed and said' 'Get your arse off this station'.

In 1991 I made my last promotional move by leaving Leeds after 20 years, to become Route Chief Trains Inspector for InterCity, based in York Headquarters. My patch now, was from London King's Cross to Aberdeen a distance of 524 miles. It was to take some time for the little lad from Normanton to get used to walking through the hallowed portals of the Main Headquarters Building nearly every day. It would also take some time to get used to escorting VIPs who travelled along this famous route, as this was also now part of my job. These were to include Her Majesty The Queen, Prince Philip, Princess Margaret, Princess Diana, Princess Anne, Prince Michael of Kent, the Duke and Duchess of Kent, the Duke and Duchess of York, and the Duke of Gloucester. If anyone had told me that one day I would be escorting these type of people along the East Coast Main Line in first class luxury, and sometimes taking the same meal

217

as them, I would have said: 'I think you are in cuckoo land. But it was to happen and on many occasions and I treasured these experiences. I also realised that I had been very lucky in my railway career in that I had always enjoyed going to work. I have talked to scores of people about their working lives and many have told me how they hated their job and hated going to work every day. I realise that I would have had a few bad days, but on the whole I can honestly say I always enjoyed going to work and doing my job and I would count it a privilege if I were able to do it all again.

THE INTERCITY ERA

October 1950: First use of the term 'Inter-City' on the Paddington – Wolverhampton service.

May 1962: East Coast introduce the 100 mph Deltic locomotives.

June 1969: All new InterCity coaches will have air-conditioning.

July 1972: First run of gas turbine powered Advanced Passenger Train.

January 1973: Commenced trials of 125mph High Speed Diesel Train.

May 1975: Prototype High Speed Train enters revenue service, Paddington – Bristol.

May 1978: Revenue earning service of InterCity 125 King's Cross – Edinburgh.

May 1980: East Coast 125 Trains increased from 8 to 9 coaches.

September 1981: Computer reservation system introduce for East Coast.

May 1982: Cheap overnight fares (Nightrider) London to Scotland.

September 1982: East Coast 125 trains covered 25 million miles.

October 1983: Selby diversion opened, reducing East Coast journey times.

March 1985: First Pullman Lounge opened at King's Cross.

May 1985: Simplified fare structure established.

May 1987: Second Class renamed 'Standard'.

September 1989: Inaugural run of InterCity 225 (Class 91 locomotive and Mark IV coaches) on King's Cross – Leeds service.

June 1990: London – Edinburgh inaugural run electric service, InterCity 225 by HM The Queen, 28th June.

January 1993: Passenger Charter becomes operative.

February 1994: Tribute ticket issuing machine launched at St Pancras and Newcastle.

April 1994: 'Privatisation' InterCity broken up into six train operating companies.

FRANK GEESON

In closing this book I would like to pay tribute to a truly remarkable man: historian, artist, poet, storyteller and friend to literally thousands of Normanton residents: The late Francis (Frank) Geeson. Normanton-born and -raised, he worked on the railways, man and boy, for most of his working life, spending much of his career in local signal boxes. In retirement he was to lose his sight but he still lived life to the full and pursued his many interests with vigour. Tragically he was to lose his life in a road accident at the age of 84 years but his memory will live on in the town for a long time to come. The following poem is just one of the many that Frank penned:

THE ROYAL SCOT

Before I tell the story
Of a locomotive's fame
I must mention first a signalman -
Paddy Nolan was his name,
Though some thought him temperamental
I remember him with pride
Because he stopped The Royal Scot
Just for me to have a ride.

We both worked at the station 'box
Where I was his booking-boy,
And on that certain sunny morn
Just apprehend our joy
On learning from the powers that were
In charge that long-gone day
That the celebrated Royal Scot
Was due to pass this way.

221

This steam loco hit the headlines
In nineteen thirty-three,
Achieving fame on trial runs
O'er those lands across the sea,
The vast Canadian Provinces
And the mighty U.S.A.
Where she clocked-up 15,000 miles
Before calling it a day.

Our Yankee friends presented her,
For doing this so well,
With a cow-catcher, a searchlight
And a clanging big brass bell;
On coming back to Britain
With those trophies pinned upon her
The Royal Scot around our isle
Performed a lap of honour.

And now this locomotive
Was approaching our town,
When a hand-signal from Paddy
Consequently slowed her down;
He politely asked her driver
If they'd take me for a ride –
'Oh yes – and bump him off as well!'
He jokingly replied.

A scene that's unforgettable
My memory reveals
Of the moment that I climbed aboard
This majesty on wheels;
Maroon paint polished mirror smooth,
Lines and characters in gold,
Burnished boiler, dome and chimneystack –
What a wonder to behold!

Allowed to touch the lever
That gave the engine steam;
To ring the bell and sound the whistle
Made my joy supreme.
I noted how the station buildings
Passed by on our right......
Too soon we reached the platform end
Where I had, to alight.

Those halcyon days of Normanton's
Proud railway have long gone,
But in the minds of older folk
Their memory lingers on.
While I survive, an incident
That ne'er shall be forgot,
Is that moment, many years ago,
When I rode the Royal Scot.

~~~~~~~~~~~~~~~

OTHER PUBLICATIONS
BY PETER KIRTON

Proceed at Caution - About his career on the railways, spanning 43 years. A good mix of facts and humour. From mixing with the fraudulent travellers to escorting Royalty. Never a dull moment!

Normanton, Grit, Grime and Courage - About a family history and the development of Normanton from a small agricultural village to a thriving industrialised town. To the old folk, it is hoped to bring back the memories of these days and to the young, a look at how we used to live.

BOOKS PUBLISHED BY
WRITE BOOKS

Levvy Taggers	Don Kirkaldy
Tales of the Undetected	Various Authors
Evie Pearson's War	Joyce Morton
Psychic Awareness thru the Tarot	Anita Sherridan
Bend the Bough Gently	Kathleen McBurney
Poetry She Wrote	Kathleen McBurney
Little Gems	Kathleen McBurney
Shared Thoughts	Alec Allen
Working For Angels	Audrey Morton

FORTHCOMING PUBLICATIONS

3 Kids, the Devil and a 4lb Pike	Stephen Boxall
Wagers of Sin	Peter Woodhouse
Nestbuilders	Joyce Morton
Our Stolen Heritage	Ron Curran